How to Stop Scrolling

How to Stop Scrolling

Ruby Ryba

Useful Books

How to Stop Scrolling

First Edition

ISBN 978-1-9196216-6-1

Published by Useful Books

66 Paul Street, London, UK EC2A 4NE, pub@usefulbooks.com

Contents

Introduction

> *"I wondered if the motto of our era should be: I tried to live, but I got distracted."*
>
> *— Johann Hari, Stolen Focus*

You picked up this book because you want to spend your time differently. Perhaps you feel like your phone controls you, not the other way around. Or maybe you want to increase your awareness and take stock of how you're responding to this ever-more-technological world. I love that you're taking the time to learn more about something so difficult and so important. Phone use is nuanced and individual, and it permeates so many aspects of our lives.

For the last few years, I've been a screen time strategist. I help people like you win back control over their time and attention. I was compelled to start writing this book after interacting with so many individuals who wanted to make this change but didn't know where to start. I was encouraged to finish writing it when the people I worked with experienced such dramatic transformations.

It made me realize the fundamental truth of scrolling:

> Anyone can change their relationship with their phone. But doing so requires intention, planning, and setting boundaries with the virtual world.

What success looks like

To be clear: you don't need to completely sacrifice your phone to get more of what you want. You only need to build a better relationship with it.

The average American spends 5 hours and 16 minutes per day on their phone[1] (which amounts to over 13 years of phone use over an average lifetime[2]). Some portion of that phone usage is intentional, important, and worth preserving. But a lot of it isn't, and that's what we're going after. By fighting back against the bit that's low-value, unintentional, and on autopilot, you'll unlock a bounty of additional time, energy, and attention to put toward whatever matters most.

There's also your brain and body to consider. Forty-three percent of us consider ourselves "addicted," 81 percent of us check our phone within 10 minutes of waking up, and 40 percent of us feel panic or anxiety when the battery goes low. Too much scrolling tends to make us feel pretty bad, both physically and mentally. Building a better relationship with your phone will help you start to feel better again.

> *"Impairments of focused attention, low inhibitory control, and impaired working memory."*
>
> *"... Neck / back pain, vision problems, and even weight gain."*
>
> *"... Twice as likely to have anxiety, thrice as likely to have depression, and 64% more likely to suffer insomnia."*

---

1. To avoid cluttering the text with loads of links and citations, I've collected them all in a single References section, which you can find at the back of the book.
2. Assuming phone use of 60 years from age 15 (a conservative starting point, considering a Pew Research Center report found a majority of parents of kids aged 11–12 said their child has a smartphone) to age 75 (the current average American lifespan is 78).

> *"Zombie scrolling syndrome... mindless scrolling out of habit with no real destination or benefit."*
>
> *"Smartphone apps usage patterns predicted workplace stress with 75% accuracy."*
>
> *"Infinite scrolling ... leads to normative dissociation—a mental absorption that diminishes self-awareness and disrupts memory."*

How this book will help

Many have tried and failed to end the infinite scroll. Why will this time be different?

My guess is that if you've tried other methods in the past, they haven't worked because the onus is always on you, the user, to change your behavior through some combination of grit, willpower, and determination.

Attempting to follow a rule like "Turn off your phone at 9 p.m." sounds simple, but it doesn't account for habit loops, addictive app design, or your ever-changing schedule. Likewise, rules like "Set a timer when you scroll" are too easy to snooze or ignore. And rules like "Only use your phone for productive things" are fuzzy lines that are hard to stick to over time. Worst of all, holding yourself to these sorts of rules requires the same willpower that scrolling erodes in the first place.

Our phones are too deeply entwined within our lives and too compellingly designed to be overcome through teeth-gritting, brute-force solutions.

You can't just "use it less" when doing so leaves you idle and bored and when the device in your pocket has been precision-engineered to be as tantalizing as humanly possible.

The process that works for my clients—and will work for you—is built on three pillars:

First, you're going to stop beating yourself up about runaway scrolling. We each get sucked into our phones for our own unique blend of reasons, and the only way to discover yours is by examining your unintentional scrolling sessions. The next time your phone use gets away from you, you're going to stop seeing it as a *setback* ("Oh no, I failed") and start seeing it as a *signal* ("Aha, here's what I can fix"). Beyond being vastly kinder to yourself—which is critical for succeeding at any sort of long-term behavior change—this approach also equips you with the insights required to start designing solutions that work.

Second, you're going to stop trying to fight the phone through *willpower* and start outmaneuvering it through *design*. Imagine that you were trying to build a healthier eating habit. In that case, *willpower* would be attempting to resist the delicious muffins at the café where you're meeting a friend, whereas *design* would be suggesting that you meet up at the smoothie bar instead, thereby avoiding the temptation altogether. Your phone is impossibly appealing, always at your fingertips, and actively trying to get your attention all day long. That's far too much to fight head-on, so you'll need to outmaneuver it instead.

Third, whenever you remove your phone from a situation, you'll fill the vacuum by replacing it with something even better. Here's the thing: boredom is boring, phones are fun, and phones *also* serve a bunch of critical utility functions. If you suddenly stop using your phone in a situation where you used to use it a lot, you'll be left with a phone-shaped hole that invariably pulls you back. The solution? Don't just *stop* using your phone but also *start* doing (or using) something even better.[3]

3. Not "aspirationally better," as in, "I'm going to stop eating delicious carbs and just eat broccoli instead," but "experientially better," like, "I'm going to stop eating carbs and give myself an unlimited smoothie budget instead."

The three pillars to stop scrolling:

1. Be kind to yourself (scrolling is a signal, not a setback).
2. Design over willpower (improve your environment and phone settings).
3. Never leave a vacuum (replace scrolling with something even better).

These pillars are an iterative loop, not a one-and-done. When you notice that you've gotten sucked into unintentional scrolling, you'll investigate how you got there (without beating yourself up, since it's a signal, not a setback), come up with a design-level solution that doesn't rely on infinite willpower, and then fill the vacuum with something even better. (You'll also support these changes by making your phone generally less appealing.) These little changes add up to a big effect; you'll soon find that your phone seems to have far less pull over you, making it that much easier for you to get back to living the life you want.

Why these pillars work

First, research has shown that any sort of addiction, from the moderate to the severe, has more to do with the environment than the person. My approach focuses on designing and cultivating an environment that's conducive to your ideal phone use, so your environment works with you, not against you. At this very moment, right now, you're fired up to make a change, which is amazing. But if you funnel all that motivation into the willpower to simply ignore your phone today, you'll wake up tomorrow needing to fight the exact same battle anew. However, if you use today's motivation to design a few small improvements into your digital or physical environment, you'll never need to fight that particular battle ever again.

Second, it's counterproductive to attempt to blame or shame yourself into growth. Self-compassion is key, and you need a process that accepts that fact. Habit change doesn't happen with a snap of your fingers. It's not always linear, and you'll have setbacks. Your motivation and belief in yourself will wax and wane. This is all okay. To stay in the game and continue making progress, you need to treat yourself with kindness. Which, to be clear, doesn't mean scrolling for three hours, then saying to yourself, "Good job!" Rather, it means accepting what's in the past, not tying it to your identity, and analyzing your slipups as informative signals that will allow you to design your future success.

Third, although there are indeed a few important adjustments that will make a difference to almost everybody, you'll also face plenty of situations that are novel and unique. This book will walk you through the most universal and essential changes, and it will *also* equip you with the process, toolkit, and mindset to deal with the unique and unexpected.

In short: this book will give you a reliable path toward building a healthier relationship with your phone in a way that's long-lasting and doesn't rely on massive amounts of willpower.

Why I care

I've been interested in digital wellness for as long as I've had a relationship with technology. My micro-generation experienced screen-free childhoods, then it all snuck up on us: a slow trickle of tech creeping into our adolescence, followed by a sudden uptick in early adulthood, and finally its pervasiveness today. In high school, when Facebook and streaming were newly rising in popularity and addictiveness, I downloaded one of the first distraction blockers for Mac, SelfControl, to lock myself out of distracting domains. At that time, however, most digital distractions were confined to our laptops, which naturally created some boundaries between those distractions and the rest of our lives.

As the digital world became more captivating and wove itself ever-deeper into the fabric of our everyday lives, I noticed that my relationship with technology was beginning to affect not only my individual life but also that of my children, husband, and friends. Something that began as a mere personal interest quickly grew into something that I realized could be of service to others. And it was bigger than just my family. I kept meeting people who felt powerless within a tech-heavy reality they hadn't opted into.

Alongside my life as a screen time strategist, I'm a former high school math teacher and mother of three who often thinks about habits, optimization, and what it means to be human. I want you, not your phone, to call the shots. As Henry David Thoreau wrote in *Walden*, "Men have become the tools of their tools." I think this holds true for many. But no longer for me, and no longer for you.

You've decided that you won't stand for this anymore. Now that you've made that choice, I'm going to help you make the change, just like I've helped everyone I've worked with in person. And now, let me tell you about Justin.

Chapter 1
3,000 unreads

"I'm like addicted, I think."

—Justin

These were the first words I heard from Justin, and as the conversation continued, I felt a bit daunted. I'd worked with many people, but I'd never met someone with over 3,000 unread text messages and an eight-year Snapchat streak, or someone who slept with their phone under their pillow so that if they received a notification, they could wake up to read it.

Here was Justin's typical day: After six hours on the computer, he'd take a break to work out, and he'd usually scroll TikTok during the 30-minute walk to the gym.

"Sometimes, I try to disconnect," he said. "The gym is probably the one time when I'm sort of off my phone. But when I pick it up to skip a song, I somehow end up scrolling."

He'd walk back home while scrolling for another 30 minutes, then wrap up work. "Alright, now I can relax," he said. "What do I do? Play video games?"

Justin's experience is relatable. He felt distracted by social media, and he felt the need to stay plugged in for both his career and social life. He'd tried the "daily limits thing." (Have you ever tapped "Ignore Limit for Today"?) He always felt better when he went outside or engaged in something that didn't require technology, but knowing this fact wasn't enough to change his behavior.

I gave Justin my recommendations on what to change and what to think about, which we'll get to in a moment. But after the call, I told my husband, "I think I just met someone I might not be able to help."

Three weeks later, I turned on my camera for my follow-up with Justin, not quite sure what to expect. Was I wasting his time? Would my strategies work for someone like him? Did I need to come up with different frameworks for different root issues or severities?

But to my surprise, Justin began the next call by nonchalantly rattling off how his phone use had improved. Here's what Justin changed:

- To avoid impulsive pickups and unwanted interruptions, he started putting his phone in another room when he wasn't using it (Chapter 4) and, most importantly, while sleeping (Chapter 3).
- To avoid ending up scrolling when he just wanted to change a song, he started listening to long-form content such as audiobooks or podcasts, and made himself some workout playlists.
- To remove one of his biggest "slippery slopes" into zombie scrolling, he deleted all dating apps (Chapter 6).
- To allow himself to read in peace, he converted his iPad into a dedicated reading device by deleting all apps and notifications except for the Kindle app (Chapter 6 covers dedicated devices).
- To create a bit of guaranteed phone-free time, he began taking tennis lessons with other people, where it wasn't nearly so easy to peek at his phone (Chapter 5 helps you determine what you want to add to your life).

- Lastly, in terms of mindset, he found the parent–child analogy (which you'll learn about in the Bonus chapter at the end of the book) particularly helpful for setting and hitting realistic expectations.

I still talk to Justin from time to time. To this day, he's managed to maintain a better balance and to adjust to life's curveballs. But I'll never forget Justin's unbelievable transformation between those first two sessions, which unquestionably showed me what I'd always hoped was true: **anyone can change their relationship with their phone if they're intentional and reflective, and if they set boundaries with the virtual world.**

Why it worked for Justin

How was one small conversation able to get Justin from "I think I'm, like, addicted" to triumph? It wasn't because of inspiration or aspiration; it was because *he'd finally started changing the right things.*

Justin applied the three pillars:

First, instead of just imploring himself to "do better," Justin used **design over willpower** by tidying up his physical and digital environments: changing where he put his phone, deleting distracting apps, and queuing up a slower style of media. He no longer needs to resist notifications while reading on his iPad, since the notifications simply aren't there.

Second, he **didn't leave a vacuum.** He started listening to longer-form media like podcasts and audiobooks during his walks and workouts, playing tennis with others in person, and reading in the evenings.

Third, Justin continues to be **kind to himself**. He still finds himself scrolling when he wishes he wasn't, and he acknowledges that during times of stress, his phone use might creep up, but he's given himself a huge pat on the back for the progress he's made and the systems he's put into place. He celebrates his wins instead of obsessing over what he's yet to overcome.

Why we pick up our phones

When we pick up our phones, we can do so either on autopilot or with intention. We do it on autopilot due to internal triggers (like boredom or uncertainty) and external triggers (like a notification or alert). When we pick it up with intention, we do so for a specific purpose: to check the time or calendar; to change the song or snap a photo; to take a call or send a message. These are our *on-ramps*, or our reasons for picking up our phone in the first place.

Then, regardless of why we picked it up, we can easily slide sideways into endlessly bouncing between alerts, notifications, and our app of choice. These are our *slippery slopes*, or our reasons for getting stuck.

Then, all of that can be made even harder to resist based on our phone's *proximity* (how close at hand the phone happens to be) and its *appeal* (how compelling it looks and feels).

When I talk about using design over willpower, these are the areas we'll be targeting:

The four domains of design:

1. On-ramps (your reasons for picking your phone up)
2. Slippery slopes (your reasons for getting stuck)
3. Proximity (how convenient and close at hand it is)
4. Appeal (how attractive and engaging it feels)

The best, most effective interventions will cut across more than one of these domains.

For Justin, one major *on-ramp* was the simple act of skipping a song, which he did a lot. Then, with his phone already in hand, his *slippery slope* was a "quick check" of his dating apps, which very often turned into an infinite scroll. By queuing up long audiobooks instead of short songs, Justin removed one of his most frequent reasons to take out his phone. And by uninstalling his dating apps, he removed his most common reason for getting stuck on it. This two-minute change across two different domains of design required very little ongoing willpower and immediately changed Justin's day. It's always easier to *remove* an on-ramp or slippery slope than to resist it.

Good design isn't limited to changing the phone itself. As Justin demonstrated with some of his other adjustments, you can also make huge progress by rethinking the setup of your home or office environment; the non-phone objects you place within those spaces; and the types of activities you choose to pursue. Some of these challenges—and solutions—will be unique to you. But others are fairly universal.

And the easiest, highest-impact, most universal change involves rethinking two critical places in your home and the moments they represent: arriving home and climbing into bed.

On-ramps Worksheet

Justin at the gym

1 Why did you pick it up?

☒ **For a specific task**
Check the time, change a song, send a message, take a photo

Did you do it and put it down, or slide into something else?

wanted to change a song

☒ **To fill a gap**
Boredom, restlessness, waiting, or "nothing better to do"

What were you feeling? What do you wish you'd done instead?

waiting for machine

○ **To check if I'm missing something**
No notification — just a feeling something might be waiting

Was anything actually urgent? How long did you stay on?

○ **A notification pulled me in**
A buzz, banner, or badge interrupted what you were doing

Which app? Did it need an immediate response?

○ **No real reason — autopilot**
Pure habit, proximity, or muscle memory

Where were you? Could you see or reach your phone?

Note from Ruby:
You can find a blank version of this worksheet in the cheat sheet at the end of the book.

(2) Design a change

It's easier to remove a trigger than to resist it. What can you change about your environment, phone, or routine?

download podcasts/audiobook for the gym (no song switching)

sign up for group gym classes where phone isn't an option

delete dating apps (slippery slope)

Consider all of the tools at your disposal:

- *Avoid autopilot pickups by giving your phone a home (Chapter 3)*
- *Use a dedicated device for specific purposes like checking the time or playing music (Chapter 4)*
- *Fill the vacuum Replace with a phone-free activity (Chapter 5)*
- *Delete apps that draw you in (Chapter 6)*
- *Disable notifications that distract (Chapter 7)*
- *Use distration blockers if need be (Chapter 8)*

Part 1

Redesign your environment

If I woke up next to a bowl of mini peanut butter cups, I can guarantee that eating a few would be the first thing I did. Your phone is on your bedside table when you wake up, it's in your hand or pocket as you go about your day, and it's beside you as you fall asleep. It would be borderline cruel to expect yourself to sit for hours next to your favorite snack and not eat a single one. And yet, you do this with your phone every day. Here's the simple rule that changes everything:

> Stop expecting yourself to resist your phone when it's always within arm's reach.

The end goal of redesigning your environment is to live more of your life with your phone out of sight and in a different room, so you only pick it up with intention, not on autopilot. Of course, you also want to make sure that it's available to you when you do need it. So, let's look at some changes you can make to your home and habits to make that happen more naturally. Beginning with your bedroom.

Coming up in Part 1

Chapter 2
Set your bedroom up for success

If I could give you only one piece of advice to significantly improve your relationship with your phone, it would be to not sleep with it in your bedroom.

> Don't sleep with your phone in your bedroom.

You already know how bedtime goes while your phone is in the room: you pick it up to double-check the alarm and end up scrolling for half an hour. Or perhaps you're just bored, and it's right there. And then, in the morning, your phone buzzes you awake, but you don't *quite* feel like getting out of bed yet, so you scroll through your friends' stories to see what everyone's been up to this weekend. Your bed is warm, and you still have some time until you absolutely *need* to hop into the shower, so you check your socials... Why not throw in email for good measure? Oh wow, you've been scrolling in bed for an hour. But what could you have possibly done differently? Your phone is your alarm, and it's just too hard to put it down and risk falling back asleep. Sound familiar?

So, you need to get your phone out of your bedroom. That means finding better-than-phone replacements for the two important jobs your phone is currently doing: evening entertainment and morning alarm clock.

The great news is, you can buy an alarm clock! You can get a simple one for the cost of a cup of coffee, or a fancy one with built-in white noise machines, meditations for bedtime wind-downs, and sunrise alarms for the mornings.

Now, let's picture your new wake-up routine. Your new alarm clock goes off; you turn it off. (Or maybe you snooze it once.) You sit up, do a few neck rolls, and go brush your teeth. You still haven't seen your phone; it's charging somewhere else in the house and hasn't had a chance to grab you yet. As you drink a glass of water, you think about whether you'll go for a run or get some tasks done in your hour before work. This might sound like a disproportionate result when all you did was move your phone, but I've seen it happen over and over with the people I've worked with. Something as simple as purchasing an alarm clock can drastically change your whole morning.

Removing cues, replacing routines

The reason I'm so emphatic about changing the environment and finding the right replacement is because *that's what makes these changes stick.* This is due to the science of how habits work.

To understand the mechanics of habit change, you can think of a habit in three parts:

1. A "cue" that sets it off.
2. A pre-packaged "routine" or set of behaviors that your brain performs in response.
3. A change in emotional state or "reward" that your brain expects to receive in return.

All sorts of stuff in your life acts as a cue for phone-related routines. The predictable failure is leaving things as they are and then gritting your teeth and attempting to willpower through the cue. That rarely works.

To make a lasting change, you've got two options, both of which rely on design: remove the cue, or replace the routine.

Tool #1: Remove the cue

One of the biggest cues for autopilot phone use is the phone itself. Simply seeing your phone, or feeling its weight in your pocket, can be a strong enough cue for you to start unlocking it on autopilot.[4] So, it goes without saying that when you wake up beside your phone, then pick it up and swipe away the alarm clock, you're *strongly* cued to pick it up and have a look.

In *Atomic Habits*, James Clear points out that if you're trying to get rid of a bad habit, one of the easiest options is to find ways to make the cue "invisible." If the notifications—or the phone itself—aren't seen, they can't interrupt you. This is an approach that we'll use whenever possible, and it's the core of the strategy behind fixing your mornings. By replacing your alarm and sleeping with your phone in a different room, you've essentially hidden all the cues for a morning scroll, leaving you free to have the morning you desire.

However, the cues around bedtime are a bit trickier to hide away, so we'll need to use a different approach: replacing the routine.

Tool #2: Replace the routine (while retaining the reward)

Strongly entrenched behaviors, such as bedtime scrolling, tend to have multiple cues. You could be cued into phone use by the action of climbing into bed, the feeling of being bored and not entirely

---

4. Even having it face down on a table has been shown to be just as distracting: https://www.journals.uchicago.edu/doi/full/10.1086/691462#d10291409e1

sleepy once you get there, the sensation of your head hitting the pillow, the sight of your phone right beside you, the behavior of double-checking your alarm, or all of the above. Any one of these can cue up the "routine" of a bedtime scroll and the "reward" of a steady supply of feel-good novelty and entertainment (or at least an absence of boredom) until you're finally ready to collapse.

You can't exactly make these bedtime cues invisible—at least, not without replacing your entire bed and bedroom. And even if you did that, you'd still be stuck with the internal cue of being bored and alert.

The solution relies on one of Duhigg's most critical (and most overlooked) discoveries: that the best way to change a tricky habit is to leave both the cue and the reward unchanged, but to replace the routine.

In other words, if you're cued into phone use by noticing it on your bedside table once the lights are out, and you get the reward of an easy evening of lazy, feel-good entertainment, you should put something else on your bedside table that will deliver an equal dose of enjoyment once the lights are out.

Importantly, both the cue and the reward need to stay the same. So, in the above example, a paperback history book would be a bad replacement, since (1) it won't work in the dark, and (2) it isn't lazy, feel-good entertainment. But replacing your bedtime scroll with an ebook reader might be sufficient, if you load it up ahead of time with fun enough books. Or even moving a TV back into your bedroom (with some caveats that we'll return to). Or breaking from media altogether in favor of a bunch of candles, an indulgent infusion, and some real-world relaxation.

You need to replace your bedtime scrolling with an alternative that's every bit as self-indulgent, silly, or sublime as what your phone can offer. This ticks all three of the pillars: design over willpower, filling the vacuum with something better, and being kind to yourself.

Changing a habit

Tool #1: Removing the cue

If the cue never fires, the routine never starts.

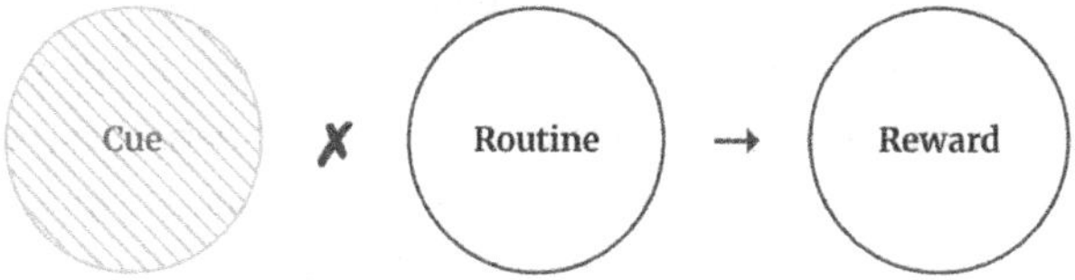

Tool #2: Replacing the routine

Same cue, same reward — but swap in a healthier routine.

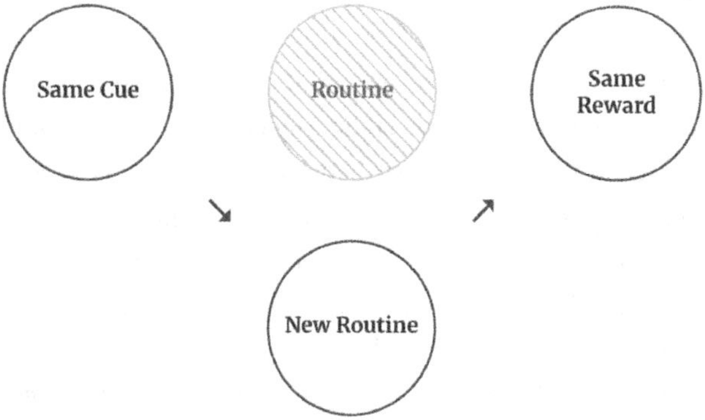

The exact replacement will be unique to you, which means that it can be a little tricky to get right. But it's also basically a license for self-indulgence, which makes it lots of fun.

Indulgent bedtime entertainment

If you're used to scrolling at bedtime, you might need an alternative bedtime activity. Or you might not. When I tell my husband to get off his phone in bed and offer him a book, he refuses the book, tells me he'll "meditate," and promptly falls asleep. Some people need more of a wind-down routine, and some people need less. You might enjoy having the same wind-down routine every night, or you may prefer having a menu of options that you get to choose from each evening.

In either case, remember that indulgence is in. If it tickles your fancy, think bubble baths, candles, and glossy magazine subscriptions. If you're creatively active at bedtime, get yourself a lovely little writing desk and fountain pen. If you're more about the ritual, buy an extra kettle and put a tea station in your bedroom. Get a record player. Renew your old hobby of flipping through comic books, pulp fiction, or tabloids. Buy a massage cushion or heated blanket. Stop waffling over whether or not to replace your old, semi-functional Kindle. Buy that cute little panda-shaped booklight or stained-glass lamp so you can read paperbacks in bed. Make your bedroom somewhere you want to be, not just somewhere you need to distract yourself from.

If you find it hard to justify the price of these little presents to yourself, consider that a good night's sleep is the best thing you can do for your health and daytime focus (and, thus, your professional performance), and that getting away from bedtime scrolling is the best thing you can do for your sleep. Plus, in the grand scheme of things, all these items are downright *cheap* compared with the value of the time and energy you're currently spending on bedtime scrolls.

Also, consider finding nighttime activities that match what you currently do on your phone. For most people, it's simple distract-me-till-I'm-tired entertainment. But if you feel drawn to your phone to look at photos and connect with loved ones, consider printing a couple of new photo books per year and keeping them by your bed. If you grab your phone to jot down a quick note-to-self or reminder, ensure you've always got a pen and notebook by your bed. If you use your phone to play guided meditations, white noise, music, or audiobooks, consider a dedicated audio device that can play what you want without requiring you to go through a screen.

Your solution doesn't have to be fancy. For many people, loading up an e-reader with some good books will prove more than enough. But be aware that they have to be *good* books, in that you look forward to continuing to read them. (I love thrillers.) If a book starts to feel like hard work, in the sense that you want to avoid it, it's no longer serving its purpose as a bedtime phone replacement. In which case, the best thing you can do for yourself is to simply give up on reading that particular book and find something better. Many of us seem to share a strange compulsion to stick with whatever book we begin, no matter how punishing. But all that does is get you to stop reading altogether. (Kindle Unlimited, the Libby app, and library books can be great for this, since it feels a lot easier to give up on a book when it never cost you anything.) There are more books out there than you'll ever be able to read in your lifetime. Why waste your time reading one that's anything short of exceptional?

Sleep, screens, and television

What I find to be magical about screen-free evenings, and I hope you find this as well, is that when I'm not engaging with screens, I'm much more likely to notice my body's sleepiness cues. If I lie in bed with my phone, I can scroll for hours even if I'm exhausted.

But if I lie in bed with a book, I seem to notice as soon as my body wants to rest. One way to think about this is that my body's sleepiness cues just aren't loud enough to be heard against the stimulation that a phone offers.

In fact, a lot of us stopped putting TVs in our bedrooms for exactly this reason. But then we brought our phones into our bedrooms instead, which is even worse. From a sleep perspective, a screen-free evening is ideal. However, we also need to be realistic, be kind to ourselves, and realize that it isn't all-or-nothing. So, if watching videos in bed is your happy place, you officially have my permission to put a TV back into your bedroom. I prefer TV over phones as a wind-down for a few reasons. A TV is typically used more intentionally than a phone. It also has longer-form content, which doesn't result in popcorn brain[5] like phone use does. Most importantly, TV doesn't serve as an on-ramp in the way that phones do. When you go on your phone to do one thing, you may realize an hour later that you've ended up scrolling through reels for way too long. Since the TV has fewer capabilities, this is unlikely to happen.

If you're wary of replacing one screen with another, you can put a few safeguards around your bedroom TV use. First, turn off autoplay (the feature that starts the next episode automatically). A study from the University of Chicago found that turning off autoplay reduces viewing time by 18 minutes per viewing session. (If you watch TV every night, that'll save you 110 hours a year!)

Second, shift the TV's color balance to be less white–blue and more red–orange. Your eyes react in distinct ways to different colors of light, and it's the blue–white that keeps you awake. If your TV doesn't have a scheduled nightshift mode, it should at least allow you to change the color balance. Since this is your bedroom TV, shift it as far toward red as it will go, and leave it

5. Popcorn brain: "being so hooked on electronic multitasking that the slower paced life offline holds no interest" (David Levy, PhD). https://www.forbes.com/sites/traversmark/2024/04/04/a-psychologist-explains-the-rise-of-popcorn-brain/

there. (It will look a bit funny at first, but you'll get used to it, and your sleep cycle will thank you.) Alternatively, you can purchase blue-light glasses. You just need to remember to wear them in the evenings.

Third, if you still find yourself getting carried away, set a TV curfew. To make this automatic (i.e., design over willpower), buy a timed plug socket that will automatically cut the power to the TV —or your whole wireless router—at a certain hour. Just remember not to be so idealistically strict on yourself that you end up creating another vacuum that gets filled with your phone.

Prepare it in advance

One of the reasons our phones keep winning the battle for our attention is that they're always there and always easy.

If you want to replace scrolling with ebooks, it isn't enough to just put your Kindle by your bed. You *also* need to make sure that it's already got a book queued up that you can't wait to read. (And that it's not out of battery, of course.) Deciding on a new book to read isn't exactly *hard*, but it's still *hard enough* that you're liable to end up turning to your phone instead. Likewise, if candles are involved in your new routine, make sure you've got a lighter. Whatever you've got planned for indulgent evening entertainment, take a moment ahead of time (i.e., now) to get it prepped. To replace a well-worn habit, you need the new routine to be just as fun and just as easy.

You'll also benefit from preparing several backup options. Think of it like preparing for a plane trip: I like to read on planes, but I don't expect myself to stay engaged with one book for the entire flight, which is why I've got other options in my bag. You want to have the same sort of backups for bedtime (and really any time). You can't know beforehand what exactly you'll be in the mood for, so having a few options handy can really make the difference between slipping into an hour of phone use or not.

Where to charge your phone at night

To remove your phone from the bedroom, you'll need to choose somewhere else to charge it.

And it's worth noting that your nighttime charging spot will dictate when you first pick up your phone the next day. If you charge your phone in the bathroom, and you go to the bathroom as soon as you wake up, that's when you'll pick up your phone. If you put your phone in the kitchen instead, you won't pick it up until you arrive there. Or if it's in the hallway by the front door, you might be able to avoid it until you're walking out the door. Consider your morning routine, think about when you want your phone to enter the scene, and place your phone accordingly.[6]

For me, I wake up, get ready for the day, get my kids ready, have breakfast with them, and only really need my phone when I head to the car to drive them to school. So, my phone charges downstairs in the kitchen, where I can grab it right before I head outside. It's also useful to have it there just in case I need to reference an email about a school spirit day during breakfast. I initially started charging my phone in my bathroom, partially because it was easier to put it there if I was already upstairs with it. However, I didn't like seeing it first thing in the morning, and sometimes I'd forget about it and then need to run back upstairs to grab it before heading out for drop-off (or realize I didn't have it only after both kids were buckled in), so I found the kitchen to be a better place for me. (The bathroom now serves as my backup spot

6. As a quick aside on phone settings (covered in detail in Part 2), bedtime is strongly supported by enabling a scheduled "Sleep/Do Not Disturb" mode that goes on every night (to avoid the on-ramp of inbound notifications) and having the phone turn itself to grayscale on the same schedule (to make videos and images less appealing and engaging). If nothing else, picking up your phone and noticing it's all monochrome can be a helpful reminder of both the time and your goal; this can sometimes be enough of a nudge for you to go put it in its nighttime spot and get started on the evening you really want to have.

on the occasional night I feel too tired to walk down to the kitchen.)

Wherever you choose, ensure that the nighttime charging spot is *permanent* (i.e., there's always a charging cable there), and *remove* the charging cables from your bedroom.

> If you don't have an alarm clock yet, try this tonight: If there's an outlet in the hallway right outside your bedroom, charge your phone there. You'll still hear the alarm, but your phone won't be within arm's reach. Even having your phone outside your bedroom for one night outside is a powerful reset. If this solution isn't accessible to you, find the plug that's farthest from reach and plug your phone in on the floor.

Applying the three pillars

You've applied design over willpower by identifying your evening and morning on-ramps, getting your phone out of your bedroom, and redesigning your evening routine. You've filled the vacuum of utility with a dedicated alarm clock and the vacuum of boredom with evening entertainment. The last pillar is being kind to yourself, which you've begun by allowing yourself to go indulgent with your evening alternatives, offering yourself options, and maybe even buying some fun new stuff.

But being kind to yourself also means understanding that your phone will sometimes still end up in bed with you, and that's okay. Especially if you find yourself at the end of a difficult, draining day, you might just want to curl up with your phone. We all have days like that. This isn't all-or-nothing, and the changes you've made to your environment and routine will still make it easier to reduce your phone use in the long term.

On the other hand, if you realize that you're never using your nighttime charging spot, even on the "normal" days, there's still no need to beat yourself up about it. Instead, treat the scrolling as a signal and ask yourself why the charging spot didn't work out as expected. Is the location inconvenient? Did you end up grabbing your phone due to some on-ramp, or because your bedtime alternatives weren't good enough or easy enough replacements? Be kind to yourself, get curious about how it happened, then tweak the design until a phone-free bedroom feels easy. If you're doing it right, it shouldn't feel hard.

And if you're worried the alarm clock won't go off, first ask yourself: Is this a legitimate worry, or does it maybe just feel uncomfortable not having your phone next to you? If you're truly worried you'll be late for work, you can either buy a plug-in clock with a battery backup (either as a single device or two separate ones). I use a plug-in sunrise alarm and have a battery-operated clock as my backup, which goes off five minutes later. The batteries need to be replaced only once or twice a year, as clocks don't need lots of power.

TASK: Create your bedtime toolbox

1. Remove the cue: Where will you charge your phone at night?
2. Replace your routine: What bedtime activities will you try out?
3. Prepare: What do you need to buy or move into or out of your bedroom?

Chapter 3

Give your phone a home

Remember our first rule? Anyone can change their relationship with their phone, but doing so requires intention, planning, and setting boundaries with the virtual world. You've already made some big improvements for your evening and morning, and now it's time to expand the same approach to the rest of your day.

The first, and most important daytime boundary is to decrease proximity by *maintaining a healthy physical distance between yourself and your phone*. You wouldn't want your friends to follow you around the house all day; that would be suffocating. Letting your phone follow you around is only one step removed from this.

> The goal is to live more of your life with your phone out of sight and in a different room, so you only pick it up with intention, not on autopilot.

It may seem like such a simple strategy, but every single client I've worked with has shown tremendous improvement with this simple adjustment.

We'll use a three-pronged attack.

First, you're going to *give your phone a home*: a dedicated daytime drop zone (or two) where you'll set it down when you first walk in the door, as well as any time you finish using it at home.

That little bit of distance will be of tremendous help in curbing the autopilot unlocks.

Second, you're going to gradually *identify the on-ramps to scrolling* that are lurking throughout your house and day, then either get them out of sight or replace them with something better.

Third—which we'll return to a bit later—you're going to adjust your phone's setup to *make it less appealing*, allowing you to put it back down more easily after using it.

Phone freedom: The three-pronged attack

1. Give your phone a home to create some healthy distance.
2. Identify, remove, and replace the on-ramps to unintentional usage.
3. Make your phone less appealing to make it easier to put it back down.

This all starts with making the decision to put your phone down (somewhere out of sight and out of mind) instead of allowing it to follow you around the house.

Decisive moments and proximity

In *Atomic Habits*, James Clear talks about the importance of "decisive moments," where one tiny behavior can tilt the whole rest of your day in one direction or another. Clear gives the example of arriving home from work and either lacing up his running shoes or flopping onto the couch: a decisive moment indeed.

For our purposes, arriving home is also a decisive moment, because it determines whether you'll spend the rest of the day with your phone in your pocket, following you around the house, or put it in a place that creates some healthy distance. And really, every single time you finish using your phone is a decisive moment, since you'll either set it down within arm's reach (where you'll be tempted to take a peek on autopilot) or return it to its proper home (where you won't).

Having your phone *over there* instead of *right here* might not seem like such a huge deal, but it is. Pretty much all scientific literature on self-regulation, behavior change, and even addiction recovery includes the use of physical distance. Beyond making your phone that little bit harder to see and reach (which Clear calls "make it invisible" and "make it difficult"), the act of standing up and walking over to your phone creates a moment of delay between impulse and action where you're able to notice your behavior—and then, if you'd like, change it.[7] You might still decide to go over and check your phone anyway, but at least it's now a conscious decision instead of pure autopilot, which is a major step in the right direction.

Picking the right drop zone

Depending on your home layout and how often you need to use your phone at home, your daytime drop zone can be the same place as your bedtime spot. Or it might be somewhere different.

---

7. This delay between impulse and action is called *latency*. Latency is the time or friction between an urge and your ability to act on that urge. The higher the latency, the more time you give your rational mind to intervene. For unwanted behaviors, you want to increase latency. (And for wanted behaviors, you want to decrease the amount of time you give yourself to talk yourself out of it.) This is one of the key principles behind why I advise you to keep your phone in a drop zone, use distraction blockers (Chapter 8), and delete apps you don't want to use (Chapter 6).

The ideal drop zone...

1. Gets your phone out of sight and out of mind as soon as you're home.
2. Is in a convenient enough location that when you do need it, it's accessible.
3. Is somewhere you can hear it if you need to be able to receive an important call or alert.

There's an obvious tension between these goals (which is why you can't just drop your phone into a time-locked Faraday cage and call it a day[8]), so you should allow yourself a bit of trial and error to get it right.

My husband decided to put his daytime drop zone way down in the basement, where he had his home office. He figured that this would let him fully disconnect and be present with his family. Great intentions, and pretty rational. Put it far away to reduce the likelihood of using it, right? But the basement ended up being annoying enough to travel to that, after needing to go get his phone once for whatever random reason, he wouldn't bother to go back down and put it back. And eventually, he stopped leaving it down there at all. This is totally normal, and it isn't something to fret over. The trick is to be realistic instead of idealistic, notice that the drop zone isn't working, then try a different spot. The only way to "fail" is to stubbornly cling to an impractical drop zone that you never actually use. Figuring out the perfect drop zone takes intention, reflection, and trial and error, and it's okay if the first attempt is a dud.

---

8. A Faraday cage is a fancy box that blocks *all* wireless signals, leaving your phone inert while it's inside. I had friends who used this approach back when we were all a bit younger, but it's harder to justify once you need to be able to receive an emergency call from your kids at camp or your clients in a different time zone.

It's also possible for a drop zone to err in the other direction by being a bit *too* convenient. Wendy, a client of mine, had been using the kitchen as her nighttime charging spot, and she decided to use it as her daytime drop zone as well. It was easy and convenient, and keeping her phone alongside her keys and wallet meant she'd always be able to find it when leaving the house. But during the day, while in and out of the kitchen with her two small children, it was too easy for her to simply pick it up as she walked by, only to realize she was staring at her phone while her kids were talking to her. Wendy and I discussed her options for other placements, but she felt like the kitchen was the best location. So, instead of changing the location of the drop zone, we hid it. The phone moved from the countertop (where it still charges at night) to the drawer right underneath. The simple shift of moving it out of sight cut Wendy's average daily pickups from 143 to 87.

> One helpful guiding principle for a daytime drop zone is *accessible but invisible*. If you're constantly walking past and seeing your phone, then your choice probably isn't ideal.

Accessible but invisible

As Wendy demonstrated, switching from a countertop to a drawer can be a good solution, especially if you're able to route a charging cable inside. The top of the fridge or a high shelf are other great choices, as you can hear and reach your phone but won't see it. Or, if you've got a mudroom, a cabinet, or another small space between the front door and your living spaces that you only use when you're entering or exiting your home, that can also be a great spot.

Your drop zone should be close enough that it doesn't feel like a chore to go there and drop off the phone (and so you can hear calls and alerts from priority contacts, which we'll discuss shortly), but it should be out of sight. Think: up high, down inside, or otherwise tucked away.

While it can be a great idea to make your phone's home official by buying a new charging zone or container to suit the spot, I'd advise against the style of stand that keeps your phone propped upright, since those are always more attention-grabbing.[9] Finding the right drop zone is a big step toward using your phone only when you *want* to use it, not just because it's there.

When you can't afford to miss that message

One of the reasons we feel so tethered to our phones is that there *might* be something we can't afford to miss: a call from our kid or partner, a critical out-of-hours work alert, or a short-notice invite from a friend.

Paradoxically, you can't put these possibilities out of mind by trying to ignore them; you can do so only by taking them seriously and making a plan that ensures you don't miss them. I suggest a two-part approach (plus a bonus tool that, depending on your circumstances, might be a useful addition).

Tool #1: Scheduled batch-checking

First, ask yourself whether you need to respond to this particular type of alert *immediately* or only *soon enough*. For pretty much anything outside of a legitimate family emergency, answering within an hour is every bit as good as answering within a minute. (And very often, answering by the end of the day is just as good as within the hour.)

If your answer's *soon enough*, you're going to use the strategy of *scheduling a time to check*. If your brain knows that you're going to scan for critical emails at 9 p.m., after the kids are asleep, it can

9. You'll remember from Chapter 2 that phones distract us even when we see them face down.

stop worrying about whether something arrived during dinner time. This even works for not-so-critical concerns, like wondering whether you got any new comments on that video you posted earlier. If you've got a scheduled time to check all your socials coming up later in the day, you'll eventually find yourself less bothered by the uncertainty in the meantime, since you know you won't miss anything.

When you start batch checking, you may find yourself itching to check for new messages. This is perfectly normal; after all, before you made this shift, you were checking much more frequently. Notice the urges, and give yourself lots of credit every single time you successfully hold off from indulging in a check.[10] Every time you do this, you're strengthening the muscle and moving towards the future you who will only check when batch checking!

Remember, the goal isn't to remove all phone use but to make your phone use more intentional. By checking inbound messages and alerts on *your* schedule instead of whenever they happen to arrive, you're interacting with your phone on your own terms. And by batching these checks into more efficient, dedicated blocks, you'll still end up saving a bunch of time and attention without missing anything.

Tool #2: "Do Not Disturb" exceptions

If, however, there are some messages you really need to get *right away*, then instead of carrying your phone around all day and checking every alert, set your critical contacts to be "Do Not Disturb" exceptions. This means your phone will make a noise even if it's set to "Do Not Disturb." (For more detailed instructions, see "Setting up 'Do Not Disturb' exceptions" in the Cheat sheet.)

Setting a priority contact is easy enough that you can even do it temporarily, like starring a friend as a "Favorite" while you're

10. If you find it difficult to stick to your predecided batch-checks, using a wallpaper to remind you or a distraction blocker (Chapter 8) can help.

waiting for them to tell you that they're ready to meet up, then bumping them back off the list afterward.

If you've got a few of these contacts, it can help to give them each a different ringtone. (And then, if you realize that you keep ignoring a call from someone on your "Favorites" list, or that you keep missing a call from someone who's not on the list, you can make adjustments accordingly.)

In short, if you find yourself checking *every* notification out of fear of missing *one* notification, consider finding a way to make that one notification louder so you can safely silence all the others.

Bonus tool: Dedicated devices

I have some doula friends who need to be available for midnight calls from clients going into labor. Using priority contacts doesn't work, since the call might arrive not just from the client herself but potentially from her partner, her parent, or even a random midwife or doctor.

In cases like this, a dedicated device is required. Some doulas use a second phone just for clients that can safely stay on loud since it doesn't contain any apps or other notifications. Other doulas dislike the idea of carrying around a second phone and use a beeper instead.

> We'll talk about notifications in detail a bit later, but it's worth mentioning that once you're confident that the important alerts will reach you, and once you've given yourself a scheduled time to check everything else, you can disable all the other notifications and badges.
>
> After all, you're going to check them all soon anyway, right? So, why do you need them popping up to distract you in the meantime?

To summarize:

- If you just need to receive a message *soon enough*, reassure your brain that you won't miss it by giving yourself a scheduled time to check (usually best for regular work, social media, messages, and everything else).
- And if you need to be immediately accessible to certain key people, use priority contacts and "Do Not Disturb" exceptions (usually best for immediate family).
- And if you need to be immediately on-call to a whole group of people, use a dedicated device (usually best for emergency work).

Healthy distance achieved

By creating a drop zone that's out of sight and also ensuring you won't miss anything important, you've used design over willpower to decrease proximity. This will significantly reduce how often you're cued into using your phone by seeing your phone, and it will also add some much-needed friction to the autopilot on-ramp of picking it up just because it's there.

You're being kind to yourself by acknowledging that you're still allowed to hear and jump up when you get a call or message from that important person. You're also giving yourself a scheduled time to curl up with your phone (if you want) and check all those other fun bits and pieces. You aren't giving anything up; you're just doing it on your own schedule, on your own terms, and with intention.

That's a great start, and I promise that if you make the effort to give your phone a home (and apply a bit of trial-and-error adjustment until you find the *right* home), it's going to make a huge difference. But you're not quite done yet. To get this change to stick, you still need to figure out how to fill the vacuum in your day that the phone leaves behind. Your phone serves a lot of functions, from cooking clock to calendar. And to start loving your life without it, you'll need to find the right replacements.

TASK: Reflect and design

1. What spot will you try first as your phone's daytime drop zone? (Remember, accessible but invisible.)
2. What can you batch-check? How often will you batch-check?
3. Do you have, or could you have, a work phone or other dedicated device?

TASK: Phone setup

- ☐ To your "Favorites" list, add contacts that you would want to hear from when your phone is on "Do Not Disturb."
- ☐ Adjust your settings so that you still receive calls from "Favorites" while your phone is on "Do Not Disturb."
- ☐ After adjusting these settings on your phone, take a moment to go put it back in its drop zone, so you can continue with your day ;)

Chapter 4

Set up the rest of your home

You can broadly divide your phone usage into three categories:

1. Autopilot pickup: you grab it because it's there, it made a noise, or there's nothing better to do.
2. Specific utility: like checking the clock or calendar, searching for a recipe, setting an alarm, or making plans with a friend.
3. Entertainment: the phone is always easy and fun, so it becomes the default option when you're looking for something to pass the time.

For the first category—autopilot pickups—you've already done the important thing: you've created some healthy distance by giving your phone a home and leaving it there.

But in addition to the impulsive, autopilot stuff, we also reach for our phones for many *intentional* purposes throughout the day —both utility and entertainment—each of which can act as an on-ramp into unintentional scrolling. (Not to mention that when you expand your options outside of your phone, you may find much better options).

To avoid needing to grab your phone quite so often, you'll use the same approach as you did for your bedroom:

- ☑ Reduce the autopilot pickups by creating physical distance.
- ☐ Replace the phone's utility functions with dedicated devices and analog objects where feasible.
- ☐ Replace the phone's entertainment with a pile of easily accessible, better-than-phone alternatives.

Remember, most phone use isn't inherently bad. If you're able to use your phone for its intended purpose—whether utility or entertainment—then return it to its home and move on with your day, I'd say you're in a pretty good place. But for most of us, thanks to the phone's design and through no fault of our own, that original purpose leads to the slippery slope of bouncing between alerts and notifications until we end up stuck in our infinite scroll of choice, losing unintentional hours to what was supposed to be one intentional minute.[11]

Everybody's day is different, so I can't tell you exactly which on-ramps will matter most to you—nor exactly how to fix them. What I can do is share a few ideas from around the house that have worked wonders for my other clients. Try to find one or two ideas that will solve a common on-ramp for you, then commit yourself to start making those changes before the end of today.

Kitchen: Clocks, timers, calendars, and cookbooks

First, put a clock on the wall. Checking the time by glancing at your phone isn't the *worst* on-ramp (since it doesn't require you to

11. How about you? Are you able to check the time on your phone without checking your notifications? Do you get sucked into checking other apps when you only meant to check a recipe? Are you able to take a photo without ending up on socials? Slippery slopes are all around us.

unlock the screen), but using your phone in that way still ends up forcing you to carry it around all day. You shouldn't have to look at a screen just to figure out how long you've got until the next thing. Ideally, you'd put a clock in every room of the house. But the kitchen is where we tend to find ourselves running late most often, so start there. (Wristwatches are great too, but the nice thing about a wall clock is that you'll never forget to wear it.)

If you find yourself checking your phone's calendar every morning, consider putting a paper one in the kitchen, too. It's generally not worth transcribing every single appointment from your phone to the wall; a paper calendar only requires a little bit of key information to offer enough of a sense of the type of day it is (school holiday, early gym session, important work deadline, etc.) to get you through your morning routine without feeling like you absolutely have to check your phone.

We also use our phones constantly while cooking. To remove these on-ramps, buy a few different types of timers (pomodoro, magnetic, hourglass). They cost basically nothing and can range from cute and fun to elegant and utilitarian. Digital timers are more precise, but analog timers (the type you twist) are a lot faster to set, which means you'll use them more often. I keep magnetic timers on my fridge and stove hood, and others scattered around the rest of the kitchen, so it's always easier to find a timer than my phone.

If you use your phone for recipes, treat yourself to cookbooks (and maybe even a nice countertop stand to keep them propped open) or borrow a few from your local library.[12] Cookbooks are big, beautiful things, a pleasure in and of themselves, and you can use them with your partner or kids to make cooking into a shared activity. (Plus, if you're the sort to scroll socials for cooking ideas, you'll get even more benefit from having a bunch of beautiful books on hand as a real-world alternative.) Or if you're more of the

12. Yes, cookbooks can seem expensive, but (1) each book contains a *lot* of recipes and lasts basically forever and (2) it's a lot cheaper than losing your whole day to FoodTok.

DIY type, start bringing back the old tradition of keeping a box full of well-worn index cards containing secret family recipes.

My personal solution is a bit of a midpoint. I use cookbooks from the library, but I also have a three-ring binder full of plastic sleeves. I print out recipes that I find online, and if I like them enough to return to them, I add them to my binder. The plastic sleeves protect the paper from my cooking and also remove the step of needing to hole-punch the recipe.

If you ever need to look up a recipe on your phone anyway (we can't account for everything!) and you don't own a printer, consider taking a minute to transcribe the necessary details onto a piece of paper, then put your phone back away in its home. That might feel slower, but it's really not—you might *feel* the two minutes of paper time moreso than an equivalent amount of phone time, but that's just because your brain hasn't zoned out into scroll mode. And once it's on paper, you won't risk falling down a slippery slope each time you need to reference the recipe.

Pay attention to your other kitchen on-ramps, and think creatively about how to replace them with dedicated devices. For example, if you grab your phone to figure out how many grams of flour are in a quarter cup, consider buying a measuring jug with all the common conversions marked. Or get a set of measuring cups in both imperial and metric. Or spend $12 on a digital scale that can simply toggle between units. There's a novelty kitchen device for literally everything. Chances are, you won't need too many, but if one might allow you to avoid repeated on-ramps into scrolling, I'd consider it a worthwhile investment.

Living room: Music, photos, and media

Music is a huge on-ramp into unintentional phone usage, especially when you need to fiddle through multiple screens and delays while trying to get that Bluetooth speaker powered up and connected. The connection is being annoyingly slow, so why not check that notification while you wait? Ten minutes later, there's still no music, and you're wondering what you were meant to be doing. The solution is to put a permanent music device where you want it. Not a speaker you still need to connect to, but something that works *without* your phone. One of my clients solved the music issue by buying a little coffee table that doubles as a speaker, plus an old, cracked phone converted into a dedicated music device. The music phone has no SIM card or notifications, has no apps other than Spotify, stays permanently on top of the speaker table, is connected by an aux cable to avoid any fiddling with Bluetooth, and is logged into its own Spotify account so it never collides with anybody else's; meanwhile, both phone and speaker are permanently plugged into a power supply, so they're always ready. Anyone in the family can manage the music without looking at the screen via the table's physical buttons, and searching for different music can be done from "the music phone" without risking any other distractions.

Another client, who had a combined living space/home office, attached a set of high-quality external speakers to her computer, complete with remote control. She still occasionally needs to open up the computer to switch playlists, but she finds that to be far less of a slippery slope compared to opening her phone to do the same. (Or if you want to go retro, I hear vinyl is making a comeback.) Some people also like controlling music with a voice-activated device like Amazon Dot or Google Home, although making your home more connected is a matter of personal preference.

The desire to take photos is a more challenging one, especially if you've got kids. Dedicated devices do exist and can be great fun, whether it's a small digital camera, a Polaroid, or a full-on analog camera. However, this is a place where a phone is hard to beat: the quality is amazing, the ability to share is just a tap away, and you get video, too. One option is to turn an old phone with a good enough camera into your dedicated household photo phone and leave it where you tend to find yourself hanging out and snapping photos. But if that's not viable, you can reduce the risk by giving yourself a rule: always take photos from the lock screen (i.e., without unlocking the phone), and never review or share them right away. If you combine this rule with *making your phone less attractive*, which we'll talk about soon (especially making a boring lock screen, covered in Chapter 6), you'll have an easier time of taking your photos without getting sucked into looking at other people's. As for when to review and share, treat it like any other nonurgent phone activity by giving yourself a scheduled time to batch-check it all later (see Chapter 7).

Finally, what about just being bored around the house? Treat it in the same way as bedtime: prepare a pile of indulgent entertainment—books, magazines, sketchbooks, comics, musical instruments, or any other hobby—and scatter it strategically near wherever you tend to find yourself bored and idle. I like to read, so I keep books in strategic spots. There's one on my bedside table, another in the playroom, and one in my tote. If I'm reading something particularly compelling, chances are, I'm carrying it around with me. But just in case I'm not, thanks to this intentional setup, I usually have a book within arm's reach.

Home office: Your computer is already enough

James, a client who worked in finance, said he picked up his phone every time a market alert came through. But when we dug into it, he admitted that the same alerts popped up on his computer. Checking them on his phone was really just an excuse to peek at less essential stuff. Together, we set up a new rule: his phone lived on a dedicated spot on the credenza behind his desk. Close enough to be accessible for a two-factor authentication or verification code, but far enough away that if he wanted to check it on an autopilot impulse, he'd have to stand up and walk over. That small shift created a physical distinction: when he was at his desk, he was working; when he stood up to check his phone, he was on a break. Within a couple of weeks, James noticed he was less distracted, and the act of standing up made him more intentional about whether he really needed that break at all.

This is true of almost every work environment: most anything that tempts you into reaching for your phone can actually be done on your computer instead, allowing you to keep your phone firmly out of sight.

Speaking of using your phone as a break from work, is that really what you want to be doing with your breaks? Or is that just an old autopilot reflex? Screen-free breaks are vastly more restorative, and maybe there's something you'd prefer to be doing with your break time.[13] If so, ensure that your office drop zone (whether home office or real office) is out of sight and off the path you take when stepping away from your desk.

Bathroom: There's a book for that

Without wanting to dwell on this point, you may be surprised to realize that your trips to the bathroom tend to go a whole lot faster once you stop taking your phone with you, to the extent that you won't even feel like you have time to miss it.

Still, if you like, you can also just leave a couple of books in there: stuff that's easy to pick up and put down. Back in the pre-smartphone era, there used to be a whole genre of books for this purpose, called "toilet reads." But these days, any easy read will do the trick.

Alternatively, consider leaving this one moment in your day intentionally empty, treating the solitude of the *rest*room as a gentle reminder to *rest* your brain with a quiet minute of unhurried mindfulness.

---

13. Your breaks don't have to be all-or-nothing. You can do both! Just as you want to eat your veggies but also indulge in some occasional chocolate, you can take a stretch break in the morning and a scroll break later in the day.

Also: Paper, printers, and sticky notes

Another common on-ramp is using your phone to write and reference reminders to yourself. The simple solution is to ensure you've always got a pen and paper at hand. I've got one client who likes to carry a piece of folded-up paper in their pocket at all times, others who swear by a magnetic notepad stuck to the fridge, and some who are never far from a pile of sticky notes. My husband keeps his reMarkable on his nightstand (think Kindle but for note-taking). An author I worked with, who liked taking audio notes, found that using a dedicated audio recorder both kept him on task and ended up being faster and easier, since he could start recording with a single button press.

If you have a home office, a laser printer is also worth considering. The ink for laser printers costs basically nothing, the printing time is practically instantaneous, and the devices themselves have also become fairly inexpensive. Once ink is "free," you can move things from your phone onto paper. Print a quick copy of that recipe you googled instead of needing to keep double-checking it on your phone. Instead of hunching over your phone to read that lengthy article, just print it out and go read it on paper in the sun.

Your new home

Inviting dedicated devices into your life is an exciting way to shape your physical environment and make it yours. It means you know and value yourself and your routines well enough to invest time, money, and energy into setting up the devices that will serve you. Almost everyone has a smartphone. Not everyone has a record player, or a bulletin board, or a headlamp for nighttime reading. But you could! Dedicated devices decorate your life, and make you you.

TASK: Reflect and plan

Think through your daily routines. What dedicated devices might help you eliminate some on-ramps and slippery slopes?

- **For photos and video:** a digital camera, instant camera, camcorder or GoPro?
- **For music and audio:** a radio or record player?
- **For reading and learning:** an e-reader, audiobook player, books?
- **For time and routines:** an alarm clock (hopefully you already have one!), timer, clocks throughout the house, calendar, paper or computer planners?
- **For notes and writing:** notebooks, voice recorders, writing tablets?
- **For entertainment:** board games, card games, puzzles, crossword/puzzle books, coloring books, knitting/crocheting materials?

Chapter 5
Fill the vacuum

I often ask my clients, "What does your ideal day look like?" Their responses often include lines like, "I would wake up in the morning and not use my phone," or "I wouldn't use my phone during little breaks at work." Although these statements are great starting points, they won't get you to the finish line.

My clients are telling me all of the instances they want to *not* be on their phones, but they're not thinking about what they *would* want to do with that time instead. If you're in this situation, you're not alone. People who aren't sure how they want to spend their time are more likely to spend extra time on their phones, as scrolling is an easy way to push off deciding what to actually spend their time (and lives) on.

It's a bit like looking at a menu and saying, "I don't want a burger." Okay... so what *do* you want? Now that you have this extra time and space, what do you want to fill it with? We've already covered some ways of filling the "little vacuums" of utility and entertainment (via dedicated devices and easy alternatives, respectively). Now it's time to turn toward the "big vacuum" of what you want to add to your life.

Think additive: Reframe your goals positively

The goal is to replace phrases like, "I want to *not* watch three hours of TV before bed every night" with phrases like, "I want to see friends for dinner after work some nights," or "I want to take a Zoom French lesson one evening per week on Preply," or "I want to read fiction before bed."

This additive framework has been found to be helpful when pursuing any sort of long-term behavior change. For people trying to change their weight and diet, focusing on the new foods they want to incorporate feels doable and can offer a sense of accomplishment, whereas thinking about the foods they have to remove and avoid can feel more restrictive and difficult.

Similarly, it can be hard to avoid taking out your phone while waiting for the kettle to boil or standing in the line at the grocery store. You're standing there with nothing to do, and that "little gap" of three minutes feels like an eternity. But if you've been wanting to find the time to add a little bit of mindfulness or breathwork into your day, you've just hit the jackpot: three totally idle minutes you can use for that box breathing you want to make time for. This is why I keep returning to the idea of filling the vacuum. It's far easier to take something out when you're simultaneously putting something in.

Deciding what to add

Start with big-picture goals: "I want to be able to play tennis socially," or " I want my Spanish to be good enough to carry out basic conversations," or "I want to retire by 45." Then, think about what can be done day to day.

Don't just fill the time for the sake of filling the time. That's what you were doing with scrolling. What lights you up? What do you love?

Aside from working toward your goals, you can also think about what brings you joy, and what facilitates your rest. Activities linked to joy or relaxation could look like breathing exercises, a jigsaw puzzle, reading fiction, or calling a friend. Activities linked to personal goals or self-improvement might look like listening to an audiobook or podcast, working on a language, taking music or sports lessons, cooking your own healthy meals, or learning to code.

Another strategy, which bridges the gap back to environment design, is to work backward: consider when in your day you're most prone to scrolling, and consider what other activity you could insert in that particular situation instead. For example, I mentioned earlier that I keep some books in the playroom. This is because when my kids are engaged in play, I don't want to divert their attention (which can happen even if I just leave the room to get something), but I start to get bored just sitting there. This really sets the stage for me to want to get out my phone and scroll; it's a scroll-prone moment for me. But with my book planted in the playroom, I actually have something else that I can do.

All of this comes down to living with purpose. What do you want to do with your life?

Start before you've made the time

Let's say you'd love to get back into pottery, join your friends for that half-marathon, or start learning how to code. You estimate it will take a couple of hours a day, a few times per week. Your phone use has been reducing, but not by *that* much. Even so, it can be helpful to commit to adding the exciting new thing into your schedule even *before* the time is fully available. Having an exciting purpose for your time will make your phone that much easier to ignore, and you might find more opportunities to cut out the phone than you had previously noticed.

For example, when I decided to write this book while still maintaining all my other responsibilities, I *had* to become more efficient with my time. Compared with my goal of getting my book finished and out into the world, the idea of scrolling naturally became less attractive. The stakes of losing my finite time to an infinite scroll were suddenly so much higher. I've seen over and over that once someone starts working toward a legitimately exciting goal, they'll have a much easier time getting their phone use under control.

The question is:

> If you had an extra 10 hours per week, what would you do?

This is a really powerful exercise, because it removes the mental blocker that limits most people from identifying what they really, truly want to spend their time on. When the time is framed as a bonus in this way (an "extra" 10 hours), it's often easier to tap into what you actually want to do, because you don't actually need to free up time to receive the 10 extra hours. (And once you find the right goal, the time will often magically start to appear as your phone becomes less attractive by comparison.)

Use positive proximity

When I asked my client Avery what she would do with an extra 10 hours, she said she would want to pursue creative outlets, especially painting and writing poetry. But she'd already tried, and it wasn't working.

She told me that she lived alone and had set up the second bedroom as an art studio, but she often found herself scrolling at her desk to take breaks when she worked from home. During our conversation, she realized that even though she wanted to paint, her phone was always closer. Walking to her studio in another room required more effort than just reaching over to pick up her phone. She agreed that this setup might be influencing her behavior more than she realized, so we decided to move things around.

Instead of keeping her art studio hidden away in another room, she now has a creative station right next to her work desk with paints, notebooks, and a candle. She lights the candle whenever she's taking a break from work. The little ritual signals to her that it's time for creative play, and she simply slides from her work desk over to the other table. In addition to moving her creative station closer, she also moved her phone's workday drop zone further away, in another room. Her new art station is technically smaller and less luxurious than her previous full-room studio setup, *but this one actually gets used.* By putting her phone further away and her desired replacement activity closer, Avery flipped the effort equation and changed the way she spent her time.

So remember: just as you've used the tools of design to remove your phone from a situation, you can use the very same tools to add in a positive replacement. Increase the friction for activities you want to do less of and decrease the friction for those you want to do more of.

Or, put more simply:

> Design your space so your phone is never the easiest option, and your desired activity always *is*.

Commit to some phone-free activities

Another client, Leon, wanted to get back into an exercise habit. After our initial call and a few tiny changes, he went from a slump of almost no exercise to going to the gym or playing tennis every single morning for three months in a row. His secret? First, he set out his pre-workout and gym clothes every night right beside his bed, while also putting his nighttime phone-charging spot further out of the way (see Chapter 2. Second, he made a simple, unambiguous rule—a bright clear line (see Chapter 8—that he wouldn't touch his phone until *after* he got back from his workout.

As a result, he turned his gym time into a phone-free environment where he couldn't use his phone even if he wanted to. He was therefore freed from the willpower drain of attempting to resist it. By combining the tools of environment design, a bright clear line, and a phone-free environment, Leon transformed his hour of morning scrolling into an hour of morning exercise, and he still got out of the house at basically the same time. In other words, he was able to find the time to exercise every single day without sacrificing anything except the autopilot scrolling that he didn't really want to do anyway.

If you recall Justin's story from way back in Chapter 1, he mentioned that the gym was the only time in his day when he was "sort of" off his phone. Until, that is, he had to change a song or wait for a machine to become available, at which point he'd somehow find himself scrolling even there. Justin didn't want to leave his phone at home, since he wanted to be able to listen to playlists and podcasts, so he used a different sort of binding behavior: enrolling in the gym's group classes instead of always exercising on his own. The social dynamic made phone use feel impossible, so he simply stopped using his phone while there.

Not too rigid

Part of the trouble with our phones is that they're able to squeeze themselves into literally any tiny slice of time, in every context or situation, while simultaneously able to expand to fill as much time as is available. Find yourself with 10 seconds to yourself in the midst of a busy wedding reception? Your phone has something for that. Ten hours of complete solitude on a transatlantic flight? Your phone has something for that, too.

Most hobbies don't seem so inherently flexible, but a little creativity can take you a long way. I had a client, Lyssa, who wanted to get back into a serious yoga practice. The intensive sessions took a solid hour, which fit into her day just fine—in theory. But whenever life became unexpectedly busy, fragmented, or chaotic, she'd end up doing no yoga at all, even if she still had several smaller chunks of time available. This is an example of all-or-nothing thinking, a common thought distortion (covered in the Bonus chapter). In Lyssa's mind, she could either fit in a full hour of yoga, or she couldn't. But in reality, if she has half an hour here, she could do some stretches; with twenty minutes there, she could work on her headstand.[14] When something you want to incorporate doesn't feel as fluid and flexible as just pulling out your phone, challenge that belief. You may be able to poke a hole in that argument more easily than you would've thought.

Another potentially perceived limitation is location. Tennis may seem like something you can only practice on the courts, but is that true? What can you do at home? Can you read tennis books, watch the pros, or practice your swing or switching grips? Would getting an extra workout in or increasing your fitness in other ways improve your play? On the other hand, Spanish lessons may feel like an at-home-on-Zoom activity. Can you use language learning apps or flashcard decks on your commute, or join conversation groups?

Beyond making your goals more actionable, these smaller variants of your core activity also creates additional flexibility and therefore resilience. And remember, you're allowed multiple replacements. You can't fit everything into every situation, but you can always fit *something*. For example, Marty Cagan is an

---

14. Take a minute to try to come up with your own "pocket hobby" like this. If you can, you'll always have something meaningful that you can do, even in small slices of time, and without requiring any special equipment or location.

extremely busy author, entrepreneur, and business leader, yet he still spends an hour or two per day walking his dog in the hills. When asked about it, he explained that he always keeps a "to-think" list in his pocket that contains his most important open decisions, problems, curiosities, and challenges. Whenever he's away from his desk but craving some mental activity, rather than busying his brain with other people's content, he just opens his "to-think" list.

Allow some little gaps

Something funny that happens when you start cooking without a phone is that cleanup afterward gets a whole lot easier. While you're waiting for the water to boil, and since you're no longer allowing your phone to occupy all those little moments, you'll find that you just go ahead and empty the dishwasher, take out the trash, or wipe down the countertop.

Phones squeeze themselves into any available gap, then expand to fill that gap up. If you simply allow these gaps to exist for a bit of time beyond that first habitual scrolling impulse, your brain will start finding other ways to fill them. This often means ticking off a bunch of those tasks that you always think you don't have time for: tidying up, starting a load of laundry, rescheduling doctor's appointments, paying bills, or ordering groceries or household supplies. There's a surprising number of things you can knock out when you set a 10-minute timer, yet the same amount of time seems to go by in a flash if you're scrolling on your phone.

These gaps are valuable even if you don't do anything particularly utilitarian with them, simply by virtue of keeping you off the slippery slopes. I had a client with a habit of scrolling while the coffee brewed before he settled into work. He'd open the phone to kill five minutes, only to realize that he'd just lost the first hour or more of his day. So, he established a bright clear line: "No screens while the coffee's brewing." By keeping that tiny slice of time—just five minutes per day—vacant, he was pleasantly surprised to find himself starting to use the time to tidy up, stretch, plan the day's priorities, or simply stare out the window and zone out. But most importantly, once the coffee was ready, he didn't need to fight his way free of his phone's grasp just to get started with work.

> If you prefer to use these little gaps for a specific purpose, you can use a technique called habit coupling, in which you introduce a new habit by coupling it with one that you already consistently do. "As soon as I have put my coffee on to brew, I will do ____." This can be made even easier by designing the environment to support the pairing. For example, I leave an empty glass next to the coffee machine to remind myself to have a glass of water before starting on my morning coffee. Think about what new habits you want to add, when (i.e. mornings, evenings, work breaks, little pockets of time, etc), and then make those activities as accessible as possible.

There's a little paradox in the fact that everyone claims to be both too busy to meditate and too bored to live without their phone. If you've ever wanted to start (or renew) a mindfulness or meditation habit, there's no better time than now. The practice of presence is the only hobby on Earth that's every bit as flexible as a phone.

Avoid overly ambitious replacements

A common tendency that sets people up for failure is to choose rather challenging substitutions for phone use. When I was helping one client brainstorm alternative activities, she mentioned "learning more about the US Electoral College." If I have a five-minute break and my choices are to scroll mindlessly or read up on the Electoral College, I think I know what I'm going to choose.

Now, I'm not saying that lofty tasks can't be on your menu. But there should be some more tempting options for you as well, especially for the smaller bits of time you want to fill. Convenience is a massive driver of phone use. As such, if you want to change your habits, you have to make the new activities as easy and convenient as possible. That includes making them visible and accessible within your environment (increasing proximity), and it also means choosing activities that aren't massive acts of willpower in and of themselves.

Your real world redesign has begun

By now, you've begun making some small but powerful changes to your living spaces. This kind of transformation is never completely finished; your circumstances, space, and self will change over time. So, refer back to these chapters (and the Cheat sheet at the end of the book) to tweak and refine your home and habits.

We'll soon move our focus to your phone itself, but first: You've probably noticed that all these changes take effort, and that there's only so much you can get done without feeling worn out. So let's talk about preserving your energy.

TASK: Reflect and design

1. What do you want to achieve? (Usually the answer is simple, and you just have to do the work. Ideas are easy. Execution is everything.)
2. What will get you there?
3. What are you interested in? What do you enjoy? (These answers can be harder to hear, so you really need to listen at every turn. If you're stumped, think joy, relaxation, and goals.)
4. What are some tasks (ideally recurring) that you often feel are crowding your to-do list?

Interlude
Energy management

> *"If you don't pay appropriate attention to what has your attention, it will take more of your attention than it deserves."*
>
> *—David Allen*

Coming up in Part 2, we're going to cover the final phase of the How to Stop Scrolling process: redesigning the setup of your phone itself, and the *digital* environment it represents.

But before getting there, we need to take a quick detour to check in on your energy levels.

Too many of us have been caught in the vicious cycle of scrolling because we're tired, and being tired because we scroll.

Even if we have plenty of time between arriving home and falling asleep, we feel too drained at the end of the day to do anything other than scroll. But this situation is an illusion. People claim to have no time for anything besides work, yet the average American watches almost three hours of television a day and is on social media for 2.5 hours a day. The time is there; it's the energy and intention that's missing.

Rather than trying to create more free time—which just ends up being subsumed by low energy scrolling—many in this situation would be better served by putting *more* into their schedules (like the activities you brainstormed at the end of

Chapter 5) and making an effort to start better managing their energy.

An in-depth discussion of energy management is beyond the scope of this book, but I wanted to share a couple of quick tips, since it really does matter.

First, be aware that your energy levels change throughout the day. Spend a few days trying to identify your "best" hours, and then:

> No scrolling (at all) during your best hours.

Protect your best, most energetic hours for your most important activities and goals, be they personal, professional, or family.

Next, be aware that sequencing matters. After getting your brain into "fast dopamine" mode via something like scrolling, it becomes even harder than normal to settle back into the "slow dopamine" mode of sustained focus. So if you're going to put some scrolling into your day, it's better to put it *after* your most important work, not before (or during).

Here's the rule (with the phrasing borrowed from Rian Doris of the Flow Research Collective):

> Flow before phone.

The same amount of phone usage, but sequenced differently throughout the day, can end up having a huge impact on both what you can get done, and how you feel while doing it.

The third and final piece of advice loops back to what we started with, and it's maybe the most important:

Take better breaks.

If you're drained after a day of work, you most likely need to insert some better breaks into your workday. Research has shown that high quality micro-breaks (defined as less than 10 minutes) improve performance, preserve vigor, and alleviate fatigue. And those breaks shouldn't be scrolling breaks. Scrolling to relieve fatigue is like drinking seawater to relieve thirst; it only makes things worse.

You can interpret "better" however you like. For some people, "better breaks" means "boring breaks," since a low-stimulation break is the fastest path to renewed mental energy. For other people, "better" means "*exciting*," where they head outdoors with their bike, boots, or paddleboard; or take the time and make the effort to go meet some friends at that new cafe. Or "better" might mean "indulgent," where you fill the bath, visit the spa, or take some you-time.

Whatever you want to use your breaks for, it should be something "better" than the status quo of staring into that little screen.

TASK: Give yourself a break

What makes sense for you? "Boring," exciting, or indulgent? Make a choice, then get specific. What will you do, where will you do it, and when? Book it, plan it, or block it off. The sooner the better.

Part 2

Redesign your phone

You've laid the groundwork by reshaping your physical space and setting up early habits. Now it's time to take the next step: configuring your phone itself. In this part, you'll learn how to quiet the noise, reduce the temptations, and set up systems to support intentional use. Think of it as moving from *designing your environment* to *designing your phone*, so your environment and phone are each working to support you.

There are two main goals here: (1) to use your phone on *your* schedule, and (2) to make your phone less compulsively attractive. We'll tackle this with a big deletion pass of nonessential apps, followed by some reconfiguration of the apps you decide to keep. We'll also dig into making your phone generally less appealing and consider settings and strategies to support your ideal phone use.

Coming up in Part 2

Chapter 6

Declutter your digital environment

There's an old Zen story about an abbot trying to choose a successor who asks each of the monks to summarize their key insights about meditation. The first stands tall and says, "The mind is like a mirror, and you must polish it diligently, every day, lest it gather dust." The next one gives a little shrug and says, "No mirror, no polish, no dust."

Your phone is kind of like that. You can either spend all day staying on top of notifications, badges, and alerts... or you can simply uninstall the apps that generate all that noise. Think of this as decluttering your digital environment: removing the cues and temptations that tend to get you stuck.

Notifications, alerts, and badges are unique in that they can act as both on-ramps *and* slippery slopes. They can get you to pick up your phone without meaning to, and then just as easily get you to forget what you were doing and click through to something else. When a notification appears, it demands that you pay attention and deal with it *right now*, like a toddler following you around the house saying, "Look, look, look!" (One of my friends named his phone Percy, and finds humor in saying, "not now, Percy.") Almost none of those notifications are truly that urgent. You can get to them on *your* schedule (set a time to check; see Chapter 7) and with intention, not simply because the app's algorithm wants to raise engagement by interrupting what you were doing. (For the ones that *are* that urgent, you can set either a do not disturb exception or a custom focus mode, both covered in Chapter 7.) And don't get me started on badges. Why does every single app presume to turn itself into another inbox that we're supposed to feel obligated to go deal with? I've already got two *real* inboxes that I can barely keep at zero. I certainly don't want twenty more of them.

Even something as innocent as an app icon, just sitting there silently on your home screen without any notifications or badges, can still be enough to cue up an old habit or curiosity and get you scrolling. Studies have shown that simply having your phone in sight, *even if it's face down and completely silent*, is enough to repeatedly interrupt your focus with thoughts of picking it up and seeing what's there. The same is true of the apps and widgets sitting on your home screen. The phrase "out of sight, out of mind" has never been so important.

There are definitely some crucial ways to optimize all of these settings for the apps that are truly essential (covered in Chapter 7). But your first sweep will use a far broader brush: deleting every app that isn't.

Does it really need to be an app?

Start with your home screen, since that's going to have the highest impact, and evaluate each and every app for deletion. Your first response might be, "What?! I can't delete *any* of them—I use them *all*!" Which is probably true-ish, in a sense.

Even if you use a given service for your work or life, that doesn't necessarily mean you need to have it installed 24/7 as a native app on your phone. Installing an app is like giving someone a private number that can always reach you. It should be done sparingly.

I use LinkedIn for work, so I naturally installed it on my phone. But the messages from the app aren't exactly urgent, so rather than allowing them to interrupt me, I set a scheduled time to batch-check them at the end of my working hours. But then I realized, wouldn't it make more sense to check them on my computer instead of on my phone, where it's easier to read and respond? And if I'm checking them from my computer and ignoring them the rest of the time, does the app really need to be on my phone at all? (I did end up deleting the Linkedin app.)

When I work through this line of questioning with clients, their first objection is to bring up the occasional instance when they're "working" while away from a computer, so they need to use their phone. Okay, in that rare case, do you actually need to check the app, or is the urge to do so just an old habitual tic? Of course, sometimes it really is necessary, in which case you can just open your phone's browser and log in via the relevant website. Sure, it takes an extra minute and can feel less smooth than a native app, but those "annoyances" are actually benefits since the friction will make you less likely to start opening the app on autopilot. (We are actually making it less appealing.)

The next objection to mass app deletion tends to be about some hypothetical vacation or road trip where they're away from their desk for far too long and absolutely *need* to remain connected to some critical app for the duration of the trip. In that case, just reinstall the app at the start of the trip, then remove it again once you get back to regular life. You can reinstall most apps in less than a minute, and you can access the content even without reinstalling them via your computer or phone's browser. Uninstalling an app isn't going to do you any harm. All it's going to do is stop it from pestering you with unnecessary notifications.

Here's a handy cheat sheet:

- If the app is important but not urgent: uninstall it and batch-check the content from your computer instead.
- If you only need it occasionally: uninstall the app, then either check it from your phone's browser or reinstall the app as needed (exceptions include boring, rarely used but important or hard-to-get-into apps like parking or banking apps).
- If you might need it in the future: uninstall the app until you do.

Here's what *doesn't* need to be on your phone:

- Anything that's a toy, a game, or pure consumption media.
- Any social media or infinite content pool.
- Anything that could be accessed through a computer or web browser instead.
- Anything you need only once, or need only rarely.
- Anything you installed while bored.

Make it less appealing

Here's a crazy statistic: when people switch their phones to grayscale (without making any other changes to their life, habits, environment, or behaviors), their daily phone use plummets by an average of 50 minutes per day. *Fifty. Minutes. Per. Day.* That's an extra six hours per week, completely out of nowhere, simply by making the phone a bit less attractive—and therefore less appealing—to look at. You can take this principle and run with it.

Every single thing about the modern smartphone has been precision-engineered to be as engagingly irresistible as humanly possible. As such, one of the easiest ways to fight back is by undoing all the clever features that were designed to keep you hooked.

Below, you'll find a few ideas. If any seem like just a bit too much, remember that some of them can be tied to a scheduled focus mode, allowing your phone to make itself automatically less attractive exactly when you want some extra help to avoid it:

- Switch the screen to grayscale (especially useful when scheduled to automatically turn on at night, along with a nighttime "Do Not Disturb" mode).
- Disable all haptic feedback from your phone, including the noise and vibration when you tap a button or send a message.[15]
- Replace the feel-good personalization of lovely lock screen/home screen photos with a simple solid color.
- Replace your beautiful protective case with something plain, utilitarian, and boring.

The final two points are a little controversial, so allow me to explain. I love a beautiful lock screen photo as much as the next person, but the more appealing and personalized you make your phone, the more you'll want to use it. Lock screen photos of loved ones or beautiful artwork make you want to pick up your phone. My advice is to set your wallpaper to a single drab color. Yeah, it's no fun. And that's precisely why it works. Mine's a gray ombre. If that's too much, find a spot on the spectrum that feels right for you. The less personalized and colorful your phone, the less drawn to it you'll be. It's the same deal with fun phone cases. You want to see your phone as a tool, not as an extension of yourself or your happy place. You wouldn't care if you didn't carry a ruler around

15. Access haptics by going into Settings, and then "Sounds & Haptics"

with you. Can you reach the same level of apathy that you feel toward a ruler? Maybe not. But a utilitarian look-and-feel is yet another step in the right direction.

Good widgets, bad widgets

A good test of whether you need a widget is to ask yourself, "Does having this widget increase or decrease my phone use?" Is it helping you *avoid* on-ramps and slippery slopes by acting as a shortcut to some critical utility, or is it making things worse by giving you yet another reason to unlock, click through, and start scrolling?

> Does having this widget increase or decrease my phone use?

At their best, widgets like those for your calendar or weather app may decrease your engagement with your phone by preventing you from having to tap around and risk getting sidetracked. By simply looking at the home screen, you know what today's weather is going to be, without even unlocking your phone. Widgets can also help you to bypass your tempting home screen apps. If you have a music widget like Spotify on your lock screen, you can tap it to get straight to the app, select your song, and move on with your life. Think about which widgets are helpful, and whether it makes sense to have them on your home screen or lock screen.

On the other hand, some widgets invite you to tap into an app unnecessarily, where the widget itself is acting as a sort of super-sized notification box. A good rule of thumb is to avoid the widgets for apps you're trying to use less often. (Another consideration: many apps have several sizes of widget, with the bigger ones including extra-flashy media and the smaller ones being more utilitarian. Go with the small ones.)

Lock screen shortcuts

Most everybody knows that you can change a song without unlocking your phone. But not everyone knows that you can also take a photo.[16] And that's not the end of it.

Plenty of useful functions can be accessed without ever unlocking your phone, whether via widgets, hardware buttons, or lockscreen shortcuts. Assuming that you've already tidied up your lockscreen so you aren't caught by a stray notification, the locked phone becomes a lot less of an on-ramp, allowing you to benefit from these key functions with far less risk.

The gestures, techniques, and possibilities aren't always self-evident (nobody ever finds the triple-click through trial and error), so it's worth doing a search to see what's possible with the gear you've got, and potentially even upgrading. One of my clients, for example, started having much easier phone-free bedtimes after getting a new set of earbuds that allowed him to navigate through audiobooks—his preferred bedtime entertainment—without needing to take his phone out of its spot inside a drawer.

Delightfully decluttered

You'll notice that we haven't talked much in this chapter about filling the vacuum or finding the right replacements. The removal of most apps and notifications doesn't tend to leave so much of a vacuum, since they were mainly just interrupting you from what

16. To make the most of the lock screen camera, consider pairing it with a rule: never review or share your photos right away. Even if you've taken photos directly from the lock screen, unlocking and tapping through to share them can drop you straight down the slippery slopes of social media and chat apps. Instead, leave a little bit of mystery by waiting to review and share your photos until your next chunk of intentional phone time, and enjoy staying present in your photo-worthy moment.

you were already doing. The big win has been in using design over willpower: instead of attempting to resist and wrangle a mountain of unnecessary notifications, you're just going to remove the unnecessary apps. Instead of trying to tear yourself away from this unbelievably appealing device, you're going to change its setup to make it less compelling. Deleting apps, depersonalizing your lock screen... This stuff can be hard. So throughout this process, remember to be kind to yourself. Earlier, I asked you to view your scrolling as a signal, not a setback. That's especially true here, and you can take that concept even further. The next time you find yourself painfully bored and craving a bit of vitamin phone, use it as your signal to start getting curious and creative about what you could add into your life design to make this particular moment less difficult in the future. (At the very least, you'll now have something interesting to think about while waiting for the craving to pass.) Designing the right solution is an iterative exploration, and you're allowed some trial and error to find the right approach. Up next: a neat and nuanced solution to the noise of notifications.

Phone cleanup cheat sheet

- ☐ Delete unnecessary apps.
- ☐ Automate grayscale.
- ☐ Disable haptics.
- ☐ Swap out personalized backgrounds and cases with something boring.
- ☐ Add widgets that help you use your phone less.
- ☐ Delete widgets that tempt you to tap.
- ☐ Use lock screen shortcuts to your advantage.

Chapter 7
Quiet the Noise

"My girlfriend told me to go on a date with my phone."

—Lucas

When I first met Lucas, he was navigating a challenge many of us are familiar with: our work's ability to access us anytime, anywhere, and how that affects our mental health and our relationships. What was especially challenging about Lucas's situation is that he lived in Boston but worked for a company on West Coast time. The result: after his workday ended at 6 p.m., his phone continued to bombard him with constant work notifications until around 11 p.m. when his girlfriend was turning in for bed.

I ran through an inventory of work boundary interventions with Lucas: Did he have a separate phone for work? No. Could he get one? Maybe. Did he always respond immediately to work messages after hours? Yes. Even when out on dates with his girlfriend? Yes. Was that necessary? Probably not. Could he consider delaying responding to the West Coast messages and having an 8 p.m. or 9 p.m. check-in time? Maybe.

I found Lucas a little hard to read. I couldn't tell how enthusiastic he was about my suggestions, whether he was feeling optimistic or hopeless, or whether he would make any changes at all. When I talked to him a couple of months later, I asked him what had been working. He launched into his progress. Here are the major changes he made.

First, he nailed the basics by creating some healthy, intentional boundaries. Given his particular job, Lucas realistically couldn't just ignore the after-hours messages. However, although he had to read and respond by the end of the west coast day, he didn't need to do so *immediately*, which allowed him to batch the messages for later. Lucas was a bit of a night owl, so, in order to maximize time with his girlfriend, he decided to wait until 11 p.m., when she would start to wind down, to knock out 30–40 minutes of work on his laptop. Having a scheduled time to check made it easier for him to ignore his phone in the meantime, and dealing with the messages in a single, focused batch meant he spent a whole lot less of his evening on work.

And then, just as he'd ignore his phone *until* that scheduled time to check, he'd also ignore it *afterward*. He removed the phone charger on his bedside table, and he started leaving his phone to charge overnight at his desk. In his words, "If I scroll at night, my punishment is a dead phone in the morning." As a result, he estimated that he now scrolls only one night a week—usually on the weekend, when he doesn't need the phone for work the next day—which he marked as a huge improvement.

Lastly, he cemented these changes by taking the time to sit down and personalize some focus settings on his phone. Alongside massively reducing all types of notifications, he set up "Focus," "Work," "Personal," and "Do Not Disturb" to go on automatically during different periods of the day. (See the Cheat sheet for instructions on setting this up.) As a result, his phone is always on one type of focus mode or another, giving him the alerts he cares about in that moment and nothing else.

Why notifications matter

Just like the rest of your phone, notifications *can* be useful (getting a message about a flight delay saves you from arriving at the airport three hours early). But so many of them are not. Non-work-related messages rarely require an immediate response, and even work-related messages usually don't require an immediate response outside of business hours. Notifications also invite us to switch back and forth between tasks frequently. As you probably already know, when you spend a lot of time switching, the evidence suggests that you'll complete tasks more slowly, make more mistakes, be less creative, and remember less of what you do. At the University of Michigan, Meyer and Kieras found that switching between tasks can cost you up to 40 percent of your productive time.

So, what has Lucas taught us?

> Control your notifications, or they will control you.

If you're responding to notifications immediately, it's certainly *not* because you're flawed, weak, or undisciplined. Your brain is functioning perfectly. Notifications are designed to grab your attention. It's a Herculean effort to expect yourself to stay on task when you receive a notification. And even if you do manage to stay on task, you're still wasting time, energy, and attention. There's still a switching cost incurred when you receive notifications that you don't immediately respond to, as your focus shifts from the task at hand to wondering if you should react to the notification. You're also contending with decision fatigue (having to evaluate whether or not to react) and finally with attention residue[17] (as you mildly wonder what the notification was about while trying to refocus on the task at hand).

How to silence notifications

You've deleted the apps you don't need. Now, let's take a look at the ones you've kept. If you're going to check your social media at least once a day anyway, do you need those notifications turned on? For the apps where you've retained the notifications, can you tone them down? Do you need the banner, home screen, and notification center? Sounds? Badges (the little red number over an app's icon)? If you're unsure, I would err on the side of less and fewer. You can always crank things back up if you realize you need to.

Another consideration is duplicate emails and notifications. Sure, I don't want to miss notifications from my bank; however, I get emails every time they send me a message, so I don't need the double notification of an email *and* a notification from the app. Choose the one that serves you better, and get rid of the other.

I suggest you start the notification overhaul in one sitting by going into your settings and methodically going through all of your apps. It will only take five minutes, and a lot of them will be quite obvious. (I need exactly zero notifications from Pinterest.) After you've laid the initial foundation, you can refine from there. Whenever you find yourself groaning as you swipe away a pointless notification, treat it as a signal to further tighten up your settings.

---

17. Attention residue: your mind's attention on a prior task while trying to focus on what's at hand. Some residual attention is natural in life: your mind may wander from time to time as you sit through a lecture or read this book. But constant task-switching greatly increases attention residue.

Adding more nuance

One crucial notification blunder is to think of them as all-or-nothing. When you're paying attention to your phone's every blink, buzz, and beep, you're doing so because you don't want to risk missing something important. But in doing so, you're also allowing yourself to be interrupted by a ton of stuff that isn't.

Toggling silent mode is too crude of a tool. This feature came out in the 1980s when mobile phones could only make calls. Your phone's capabilities have advanced tremendously. So should your defenses against their interruptions. Even disabling notifications on a per-app basis is still far from ideal, as not all notifications are equal. Within Slack, for example, a direct message from your boss might carry a very different priority than a public message in a team-wide channel. You might want the Slack message from your boss to interrupt you and for everything else to stay silent. And even then, you may want to allow that interruption only at certain times of day.

This probably sounds like an annoyingly large amount of fiddly customization. And truthfully, on a per-app basis, it can be. Which is exactly why we began by uninstalling everything that didn't really need to be there. The apps that are still present are important to your work and life, which makes them worthy of some care and calibration.

> Here's a simple rule: nothing is allowed to appear on your phone *unless it's at a time when you want to receive that particular type of interruption.*

For example, I *always* want to be interrupted by a call from immediate family, so I set those contacts as priority exceptions that will always sound, even at night.

I *sometimes* want to be interrupted by a call or message from work or friends, so I set automated focus modes to allow certain types of messages, within certain apps, to interrupt me at certain times of day.

I pretty much *never* want to be interrupted by anything else, so everything that remains stays silent regardless of what mode my phone is in; I get to them whenever I do my next batch check.

So when making your adjustments, ask yourself, "is this app/notification an "always," "sometimes," or "never"?

Automate your focus modes

Both iOS and Android provide easy access to at least three automated modes: sleep, focus, and default. These allow you to change which types of notification you receive at which times, which can be a huge design-level improvement to your day. Manually switching into these modes is somewhat helpful, but setting an automated schedule is even better. The idea is to set the focus modes to align with recurring situations in your daily life—such as work, family time, or winding down before bed—and then never think about them again.

Sleep mode should be the most severe, eliminating all notifications (except calls from immediate family members), hiding all notifications and badges, switching your phone to grayscale, and basically turning your phone into an inanimate brick. Schedule sleep mode to start a couple of hours early: not at the time you expect to be falling asleep, but at the time when you want to stop using your phone and start engaging in your new routine.

The focus mode schedule doesn't need to be exactly the same as your workday (and could just as easily be used for family focus instead of work focus), but it should represent the times when you want your attention to be the most proactive and pristine. If you use focus mode in relatively short, intense bursts to protect certain critical hours, it can be every bit as stringent as sleep mode. Alternatively, if focus mode is something you want to use for the whole workday, you might make it more moderate. Remember, an app can be *important* without needing to be *immediate*. If you're going to batch-check something often enough to avoid potential disaster, you can still leave the notifications off. (Or even just remove it from your phone and use your computer instead.)

An app can be *important* without needing to be *immediate*.

When designing your morning routine (Chapter 2), consider covering the morning hours with an uninterrupted transition between the end of sleep mode and the start of focus mode. Sure, it's a time that's technically neither sleep nor work, but that doesn't mean your day will benefit from allowing a bunch of social media to squeeze itself into your head before you've even started work.

Default mode is for the rest of your life: weekends, afternoons, and evenings. Depending on how you like to work, you might even choose to switch from focus to default mode sometime around lunch, allowing the back half of your workday to be a bit more relaxed and open to inbound alerts. Of course, even default mode shouldn't allow free rein for interruptions. You're reading this book to stop scrolling and start living more of your life with your phone out of sight and off your mind. Even in default mode, inbound interruptions should still be few and far between.

(For detailed instructions, see "Focus modes" in the Cheat sheet.)

How to handle notifications

	Could wait to respond	Must be immediate
Important	**Batch checking**	**Do Not Disturb exception***
Not important	**Disable and ignore**	*(No such thing)*

** Or send it to a dedicated device*

Make the right exceptions

Back when we talked about choosing your daytime drop zone (Chapter 3), I mentioned the importance of ensuring that you won't miss anything truly important (which is necessary to get your phone not just out of sight but also out of mind).

We mentioned three tools:

1. Scheduling a time to batch check, so you'll catch important messages soon enough
2. Setting certain important people as "Do Not Disturb" mode exceptions
3. Putting yourself on-call via a work-specific dedicated device (like a second phone or a beeper)

When following the procedures in this chapter and adjusting your notifications, make sure to keep these three tools in mind. Remembering that you'll batch check your emails for example, might make you realize that you can silence email notifications, or remove the app completely.

Badges aren't better

Although a badge (i.e., the little number over an app's icon) doesn't get in your face with distracting content, it still creates an open loop of wondering what the associated message is. For some people, a badge is a temptation, like an unopened present. For others, it's a stressor, like an unprocessed inbox. But either way, it's on your mind. After all, what if it's fun? Or what if it's important? And, I mean, you'll have to deal with it *sometime*, right...? So why not right now?!

Badges can help to remind you to check apps you rarely use, but otherwise, turning most badge notifications off will reduce unnecessary taps. For example, my badge notifications are off for messages, as I check them frequently enough. The badge only prompted me to tap into messages unnecessarily, even when I wasn't in a position to properly respond. On the other hand, I rarely use Facebook Messenger, except to stay in touch with a few international friends who I don't text. I therefore leave the badge on for Messenger to notify me if a message is there.[18]

> If you tap into an app due to a badge but don't do anything to process, respond to, or deal with what it's telling you, that app probably doesn't need the badge in the first place.

Go back into the Settings app to adjust your badges. You probably have notifications turned on for only a few apps at this point. Of those apps, which ones do you really need badges for? Turn off any unnecessary ones.

Your phone, but calmer

With notifications tamed, you'll find that your phone is much quieter, and spends more time in your pocket, without the risk of missing the bits that really matter. This is a straightforward example of design over willpower, since nobody can expect to ignore their phone when it's actively pinging them. Remember, also, to be kind to yourself; you won't dial in the perfect notification settings on the first try, and that's okay.

The settings and techniques covered throughout the last two chapters—decluttering and quieting—are the most impactful piece of phone setup, and you'll likely get a huge amount of benefit from

18. I initially turned off all badges, but realized that with messenger, I would sometimes miss a message for weeks. Trial and error, always, until you find what works for you.

putting even just some of it into practice. However, if you still find yourself scrolling more than you'd like, the next chapter will give you the tools for dealing with even the most impossibly tempting, hard-to-resist apps.

TASK: More cleanup!

- ☐ Turn off unnecessary notifications.
- ☐ Set up focus modes.
- ☐ Turn off unnecessary badges.

Chapter 8
Use guardrails and bright clear lines

Sometimes, even after you've decluttered your home screen, muted notifications, and set up focus modes, certain distracting apps still pull at your attention. Distraction-blocking apps are your allies here, one of several types of "guardrails" you can put around your phone use to provide an extra layer of protection. If you want to create a bit of extra friction between yourself and TikTok, you might uninstall the app. But if you want to add a guardrail, you might also ask a friend to change your password and keep it secret.

Distraction blockers

Here are examples of apps that help you set intentional boundaries around your screen usage:

- Clearspace: Designed specifically to help reduce impulsive app use, it intercepts your attempt to open a distracting app and prompts you to pause and reflect before continuing
- Freedom: Allows you to block distracting websites and apps for specified periods. Great for sustained focus sessions
- Forest: Gamifies productivity by planting virtual trees when you're off your phone

Download one or two distraction blockers[19] and experiment with them. Think about which apps or websites you tend to gravitate toward when you're procrastinating or bored, then block or limit those apps. I personally find that after putting a distraction blocker on an app for a couple of weeks, the instinct to check it starts to totally fade away.

Incorporating these blockers will build your awareness of your habits, strengthen your self-control muscles, and gradually reshape how you use your phone.

Delete your "drug of choice"

I'm always reluctant to use the word *addiction* about phones. As we've seen, phone use is nuanced and multifaceted, and a fairly large portion of that usage is the result of convenience and context rather than any real *compulsion*. That being said, there very well might be one particular app with an unusually strong pull over you, which you feel like you *have* to check.

This "app of choice" is almost always an infinite pool of content, and it's very often some form of social media; this means there's always something there to suck you in, even in the absence of a notification. Think TikTok, X (formerly Twitter), and Tinder. Sometimes, it's a silly little game or a fun and fast-paced group chat. The app is different for each person, but you probably know the one I mean. It's got its claws in you in a way that can feel almost physically painful to ignore.

Within the field of addiction recovery, there's a concept called your *drug of choice,* which refers to the substance or activity that presses your particular buttons in such a way that it becomes impossible to resist. In this kind of situation, neither moderation, compromise, nor logic will be enough. The only solution is to

19. The apps from the above list are: https://clearspace.today, https://freedom.to, and https://www.forestapp.cc. The particular apps available will change over time, but you should be able to find something that fits your needs.

make the hard decision to delete it, ditch it, and abstain from it. In the case of booze, that means emptying the house of alcohol and not buying any more. In the case of your phone, it means deleting that particular app, even though you love it, and potentially even asking a trusted friend to change your password and keep it secret (maybe for a month). If you're in this situation right now, I really do understand how hard this sounds. But the harder it seems, the more beneficial it will be. And the best time to do it is sometime like now, when you aren't already stuck in it.

If your app of choice is necessary for work—like social media for an audience-builder or market alerts for a day trader—it's probably still correct to get it off your phone. In those cases, however, remember to be kind to yourself by ensuring that (1) the necessary content is available throughout your working hours via your computer or a dedicated work device, and (2) you've allowed yourself a frequent set of scheduled times to check the app throughout the day.

When an app has that much of a hold over you, it's no longer just an app but a moderate behavioral addiction. There's no adequate, equivalent replacement with which to fill the vacuum, so the best move is just to put it out of sight and out of reach until your brain adjusts. And it will.

> Remember: the stronger the pull, the greater the freedom.

Bright clear lines

Some behavioral rules are vague and fuzzy, like "I'll try to use my phone less."

Others are clear, concrete, and unambiguous, like "I don't pick up my phone until after breakfast."

The second type of rule—the bright clear lines—are better. When a rule is fuzzy, you're constantly burning willpower to interpret the scenario, evaluate the rule, and justify your behavior. When a rule is concrete, it just is. If you've got kids, you already know the difference between "I think it's about time for your bath soon, right?" and "It's bath time." Somewhat counterintuitively, the more concrete the rule, the easier it is to follow.

And in many cases, a good rule can be every bit as effective as any other guardrail.

A few examples:

- No phone at—or on—the dinner table (or even in any social scenario with others)
- No phone before breakfast (or before exercise or any other part of your morning routine)
- Flow before phone (or create before consume)
- No phone after 9 p.m. (or once the kids are back from school, or whenever)
- No phone on Sundays (i.e., digital Sabbath), or for a certain half-day, or any other break

These might sound pointlessly stringent, but there's a strong analog in the folksy common wisdom about alcohol: "Never drink alone," "Never before noon," "Always with a meal," and so on. You'll notice that these rules—which have worked well enough to become accepted as social norms—are all bright clear lines. Whereas fuzzy aspirations like "Always in moderation" have been universally ignored.

An alternative structure is to rephrase your bright clear lines not as rules but as a part of your identity. So, the rule against using phones at the dinner table instead becomes "I'm the sort of person who doesn't use their phone during meals." One is about behavior;

the other is about identity. This reframing can be very powerful, because following the desired behavior brings you closer to becoming the person you want to be.

Be kind to yourself

> *Knowledge is important, but only if we're being kind and gentle with ourselves as we work to discover who we are.*
>
> *—Brené Brown*

Remember all the stuff we talked about for your new bedtime routine (Chapter 2)? About choosing something easy, fun, indulgent, luxurious, frivolous, relaxing, and meaningful? More than anywhere else, that matters here, too.

The more stuck together you've become with some aspect of your phone, the more it's going to sting to pull yourself away. But if you want a lasting change, it would be counterproductive to try to grit your teeth and muscle through. That never works. At least, not for long. The right move is to design a way to make it easier, which means adding a bunch of nice stuff back into your life, even if it feels a bit over the top. It won't necessarily cause the separation anxiety to disappear right away, but it will certainly make it easier for you to reach the other side.

Conclusion

> *Your life does not get better by chance, it gets better by change.*
>
> *—Jim Rohn*

First things first, I want to acknowledge the tremendous work you've put into this process. You've measured your baseline, reflected on areas of focus, started setting boundaries with your phone by creating physical space and quieting notifications, and taken steps to prioritize your sleep, work, and joy. The rest of your journey forward will deepen your intention, refine your redesigned physical and digital environments, and strengthen the strategies you've gained.

As you approach the end of this book, I invite you to take a moment to pause and consider what you've accomplished. Now is also a good time to make any additional adjustments you've been meaning to (has your phone found a charging station outside of your bedroom?).

Remember that your relationship with your phone will most likely be a lifelong one. Just as you have peaks and valleys in your relationships with your significant other, friends, and family members, you'll have peaks and valleys in your relationship with your phone.

How you feel about your phone today—positive or negative, optimistic or hopeless—isn't how you'll always feel. As they say, for better or for worse, this too will pass. We humans tend to forget this, though, and our current mood state acts as an anchor for all of our perceived moods in the future and in the past. (You'll notice that when you recount a memory when you happen to be in a poor mood, you may portray it in a much harsher light than when you remember it in a positive mood.)

So, if you feel optimistic and positive about your relationship with your phone use, and if you feel like you have it in the bag, that's fantastic; ride the wave! I wish I could take full credit and say, "Now that you've read my book, you'll have a perfectly balanced relationship with your phone. Forever." But that's not how it works. Many new and addicting apps will come out. You may notice an uptick in your tendency to scroll mindlessly when going through busier or more stressful seasons of life, or you may suddenly find yourself comparing yourself to others on social media after making a life decision that you're still wrapping your mind around.

And a bit of advice for when you're feeling more negative about your relationship with your phone:

> Approach what's going on with curiosity, not criticism.

As Walt Whitman wrote, "Be curious, not judgmental."

What's happening? Are you actually using your phone more, or are you beating yourself up because you're stressed about something else? Are you just plain tired? Is this a phase that's maybe okay? Or is there a driver that's changed your phone use in a way that isn't acceptable and that you want to change?

If you decide to make a change, remind yourself that you *can* do this. My work has proven to me that *anyone* can change their relationship with their phone if they're intentional and reflective, and if they set boundaries with the virtual world.

What have you accomplished? Write it all down, and give yourself a pat on the back! We're so used to thinking about what's yet to be done that we forget to acknowledge all that we've accomplished.

As long as you take the time to examine the nuance, you can make the changes you want. It isn't always easy, but it can always be done. Living in this modern, technological world, most of us can't (and probably don't want to) just abstain completely from phone use, and picking apart when your phone is serving you from when it isn't takes effort, planning, and intention. You've got this.

A marathon, not a sprint, as they say.

And if you'd like a little reminder about anything we've covered, or further discussion about mindset and more, check the Appendix for a cheat sheet, checklists, and a bonus chapter.[20] For updates and advice on the ever-changing landscape of how we use our phones, connect with me at https://howtostopscrolling.com.

20. You can also find printable versions of the cheatsheets, checklists, and worksheets at https://howtostopscrolling.com

Appendix

Cheat sheet and reference

The fundamental truth of scrolling

Anyone can change their relationship with their phone. But doing so requires intention, planning, and setting boundaries with the virtual world.

The three pillars to stop scrolling

1. Be kind to yourself (scrolling is a signal, not a setback)
2. Design over willpower (improve your environment)
3. Never leave a vacuum (replace scrolling with something even better)

The four domains of design

1. On-ramps (your reasons for picking your phone up)
2. Slippery slopes (your reasons for getting stuck)
3. Proximity (how convenient and close at hand it is)
4. Appeal (how attractive and engaging it feels)

On-ramps Worksheet

① Why did you pick it up?

○ **For a specific task**
Check the time, change a song, send a message, take a photo

Did you do it and put it down, or slide into something else?

○ **To fill a gap**
Boredom, restlessness, waiting, or "nothing better to do"

What were you feeling? What do you wish you'd done instead?

○ **To check if I'm missing something**
No notification — just a feeling something might be waiting

Was anything actually urgent? How long did you stay on?

○ **A notification pulled me in**
A buzz, banner, or badge interrupted what you were doing

Which app? Did it need an immediate response?

○ **No real reason — autopilot**
Pure habit, proximity, or muscle memory

Where were you? Could you see or reach your phone?

② Design a change

It's easier to remove a trigger than to resist it. What can you change about your environment, phone, or routine?

Consider all of the tools at your disposal:

- *Avoid autopilot pickups by giving your phone a home (Chapter 3)*
- *Use a dedicated device for specific purposes like checking the time or playing music (Chapter 4)*
- *Fill the vacuum Replace with a phone-free activity (Chapter 5)*
- *Delete apps that draw you in (Chapter 6)*
- *Disable notifications that distract (Chapter 7)*
- *Use distration blockers if need be (Chapter 8)*

Simple rules to keep phone use in check

- Stop expecting yourself to resist your phone when it's always within arm's reach
- Don't sleep with your phone in your bedroom
- Select a daytime drop zone for your phone that's accessible but invisible
- Decide on what to batch-check (email is a great start) and how often

Shopping list

Must-haves

- [ ] Alarm clock
- [ ] Wristwatch and/or clocks around the house

Time Management, Notes, Planning

- [ ] Timer or hourglass
- [ ] Paper planner or notepad
- [ ] Paper tablet (e.g., reMarkable)
- [ ] Whiteboard or corkboard
- [ ] Sticky notes
- [ ] Desk or wall calendar
- [ ] Printer

Entertainment and learning

- ☐ Books, magazines, newspapers
- ☐ Music device(s) – MP3 player, turntable
- ☐ E-reader (e.g., Kindle)

Hobbies

- ☐ Digital or instant camera
- ☐ Photo printer
- ☐ Hobby supplies (knitting, painting, origami, scrapbooking, puzzles, sports equipment, etc)

Three components of a habit

1. A "cue" that sets it off
2. A pre-packaged "routine" or set of behaviors that your brain performs in response
3. A change in emotional state or "result" that your brain expects to receive in return

To make a change: remove the cue, or replace the routine.

Safeguards for bedroom TV use

1. Turn off autoplay
2. Shift the color balance to be less white–blue and more red–orange
3. Set a curfew

Bedtime toolbox

1. Remove the cue: Where will you charge your phone at night?
2. Replace your routine: What bedtime activities will you try out?
3. Prepare: What do you need to buy or move into or out of your bedroom?

Phone freedom: The three-pronged attack

1. Give your phone a home
2. Identify, remove, and replace the on-ramps to unintentional usage
3. Make your phone less appealing to make it easier to put it back down

The ideal phone drop zone

1. Gets your phone out of sight and out of mind as soon as you're home
2. Is in a convenient enough location that when you do need it, it's accessible
3. Is somewhere you can hear it if you need to be able to receive an important call or alert

During the day, your phone should be *accessible* but *invisible*.

Three categories of phone pickups and how to address them

1. Autopilot pickup → Give your phone a home
2. Specific utility (like checking the clock or calendar) → Replace with dedicated device
3. Entertainment → Replace with easily accessible, better-than-phone alternatives

Guidelines for activities to replace scrolling

- Frame your goals positively
- Start before you've made the time
- Make the desired activity easier than picking up your phone
- Have multiple replacements
- Don't be overly ambitious – choose things you enjoy

Setting up "Do Not Disturb" exceptions

1. Open settings
2. Tap "Focus"
3. Select "Do Not Disturb"
4. In "Allow Notifications," select "people"
5. Under Phone Calls, toggle "allow calls from" to "Favorites"
6. Open Phone app, tap favorites, make sure you like the list

Phone redesign

☐ Choose a blank home screen and lock screen

☐ Delete all apps you don't need

☐ Disable all notifications unless absolutely necessary

☐ Disable badges

☐ Turn on grayscale (at least sometimes)

☐ Disable haptic feedback

☐ Use a boring, utilitarian phone case

☐ Use widgets only if they *decrease* your phone engagement

☐ Use lock screen shortcuts to interact with phone, music player, etc. without unlocking your phone

App deletion rules

- If the app is important but not urgent: uninstall it and batch-check the content from your computer instead
- If you only need it occasionally: uninstall the app, then either check it from your phone's browser or reinstall the app as needed (exceptions include boring, rarely used but important or hard-to-get-into apps like parking or banking apps)
- If you might need it in the future: uninstall the app until you do

Focus modes

Set up Sleep mode:

- On iPhone: Open Settings and tap Focus > Sleep
- On Google Pixel: Open Settings and tap Modes

- On Samsung phones: Open Settings and tap Modes and Routines
- **People:** Accept notifications only from the contacts you need to hear from immediately
- **Apps:** Don't allow any apps
- **Schedule:** Set this mode to begin two hours before you go to bed, and extend into the first few hours of your morning

Optionally, set up additional modes:

- Focus/Work mode: Allow only the apps and contacts you need, during work hours
- Do Not Disturb: Disable all notifications. Toggle this mode manually when you need to be completely uninterruptible

To make sure you don't miss anything important

1. Schedule a time to check your phone so you'll catch important messages soon enough
2. Set certain important people as "Do Not Disturb" mode exceptions
3. Put yourself on-call via a work-specific dedicated device (like a second phone or a beeper)

Distraction blockers

- Clearspace
- Freedom
- Forest

Examples of bright clear lines

- No phone at—or on—the dinner table (or even in any social scenario with others)
- No phone before breakfast (or before exercise or any other part of your morning routine)
- "Flow before phone"/"create before consume" (i.e., you do your core creative work prior to checking any inbound messages or other people's content)
- No phone after 9 p.m. (or once the kids are back from school, or whenever)
- No phones on Sundays (i.e., digital Sabbath), or for a certain half-day, or any other break

Bonus Chapter

Your phone, your brain, and you

Oftentimes, the right mindset and mental model can be every bit as important as the right environment or phone setup. This bonus chapter covers a few of the ways of thinking that have proven most useful to my clients.

The parent and the child

I like to think that in all of us, there lives a parent and a child. The "parent" you thinks rationally and in the long term. They ensure you get enough sleep, brush your teeth at night even when you're tired, and start working on projects before their deadlines. The "child" you lives in the moment and wants immediate gratification; they might impulse-buy something that looks fun, stay up late binge-watching shows, eat some junk food for instant pleasure, or buy snacks at the checkout. In terms of healthy habits, when I'm on my A game, I can parent myself better, but when I'm getting tired, the child me might kick in.

To live a balanced, fun, and fulfilling life, you need both parent and child. Parent you keeps you on track for your long-term financial, career, and health goals. Child you loves to enjoy life. But child you also loves to scroll on your phone.

So, how do you handle that? In a couple of ways. First, you want to set the child up for success by setting healthy boundaries when you're your parent self. Second, you want to accept and love your child self and see them from a place of understanding, not shame and ridicule. I often see the parent not setting the child up for success, then shaming the child.

You also want to get to know yourself as both parent and child. Are you more often a caring and supportive parent, or are you more critical? Are you a playful child? Are you compliant or rebellious? You'll probably see all of these tendencies and others pop up at different times. How you were parented also likely affects how you parent yourself.

Finally, accepting that there's a child you in the first place is very important. Kids will be kids, and there's a kid in there. So, there may be a certain amount of childishness that you'll have to tolerate, accept, and even love. If you scroll for 10 minutes at the end of the day, maybe you can say, "Well, I'm really tired, so child me wanted to scroll for a bit. That's okay."

You're not looking for perfection. You're looking for "good enough" and positive change. Small tweaks can make big improvements. Let the child play.

What scrolling is really costing you

> *You don't need more time in your day. You need to decide.*
>
> *—Seth Godin*

The screen time that shows up on your phone is very tangible: x number of minutes spent on your phone (minus the necessary moments, of course) that could have been spent hacking down your to-do list, progressing toward your goals, enjoying hobbies, spending time with loved ones, relaxing, or sleeping. But your phone can cost you in other ways than just your time.

When you spend every free moment on your phone, you don't get to decide what you're going to think about. If I start scrolling and see influencer moms getting started on their fall decorations, my mind will naturally start thinking about my fall decorations (or, rather, my lack of them). This creates a new problem or stressor in my mind that wouldn't have even existed had I not happened upon this content on my phone. So now, on top of whatever else I have going on that day, I'm suddenly wondering if I need to buy couch throws with ghosts on them for Halloween. We also frequently see upsetting news, often accompanied by graphic videos. Of course, if staying up to date on news is important to you, it's something you should do. But I advise you to schedule time to do so (Austin Kleon mentions in *Keep Going: 10 Ways to Stay Creative in Good Times and Bad* that he reads the entire paper every Sunday, and leaves it at that), or at least be mindful about when to consume the news knowing that you may come across stimulating or upsetting stories. In 1852, Henry David Thoreau complained in his diary that he'd started reading a weekly newspaper and that it was distracting him from his life and work. "It takes more than a day's devotion to know and to possess the wealth of a day," he wrote. "To read of things distant and sounding betrays us into slighting these which are then apparently near and small." He decided his attention was too valuable, and he stopped reading the newspaper.

We're in an era of constant content consumption, where if we're not consuming content, we don't know what to do with ourselves. But if the only thing we're doing is consuming content, we never have any opportunities to think or to be ourselves. I'm sometimes guilty of this myself. When I'm driving, I'm almost always listening to an audiobook or a podcast, or talking to a friend on the phone. There's nothing wrong with listening to an audiobook or podcast, or talking to a friend on the phone, while driving. But what we should avoid is feeling that this is necessary and *always* doing so, on autopilot, rather than intentionally deciding, "I want to call this friend" or "I just want to zone out a little and let my thoughts wander while I drive right now."

You might say, "Well, people used to (and some still do) read books. Now, we get our information from TikToks. What's the difference? The TikToks are actually more efficient, since I get what I need in 15 seconds." But there *is* a very big difference. When you read a book, you choose which book you want to read, you begin reading it, and if you enjoy it or find it useful or thought-provoking, you continue to read it. But if you don't, you put it down. (This logic can even be applied to TV, which I strongly prefer to scrolling due to its longer form and less frequent interactions with algorithmic viewing suggestions.) With the bite-size content, usually in video format, that we're consuming now, we have very little control over what we're consuming. The next video begins before we even realize that the one we've been watching is over. (Not to mention the new research that's been finding just how detrimental short form video is to our minds and mental health.)

Just because everyone else scrolls, does that mean you should, too?

If everyone else seems to always be on their phones, can phone use really be that bad? The idea that something is correct because most or all people believe that to be true is called the "appeal to popularity" fallacy (or *argumentum ad populum*).[21] Advertising often relies on *argumentum ad populum*, persuading viewers to consume or adopt a product because lots of other people use it rather than promoting any actual merits of it.

The problem with the appeal to popularity fallacy is the assumption that other people know what they're doing. We're all susceptible to this fallacy. Humans are social creatures, and we're affected by *mimetic desire* (when we see other people doing, having, or wearing something, we start to want it too). That's how the dad sneakers that you found so ugly at first sight eventually

21. The idea that something is incorrect because few people believe it also applies.

made their way into your closet. Mimetic desire is mostly harmless when it comes to fashion (although it certainly contributed to the rise of fast fashion), but it's something to consider more carefully when it affects how you spend hours of your time and the content and influence you're consuming. The problem with mindlessly adapting the behaviors of others is that those behaviors may not actually be aligned with your values. For example, a high schooler might use AI as a homework helper because their friends do, not considering the potential risks of regularly chatting with a bot that feels human but isn't.[22]

Most people don't know what they're doing with their phones

Remember when you became an adult, and you realized that your parents might not actually know as much about personal finances as you thought, or that many managers are just winging it and have never had any leadership training, or that almost no one can explain what every word on an insurance bill means?

Humans don't know everything about everything. Some people are experts in their field, but they *still* don't know everything about their field. So how could everyone around you be totally in the know on the best phone use practices, especially considering that smartphones only rose in popularity in the early 2010s,[23] and that everyone's uses for and reactions to their phone use are different?

Using your phone to best suit your needs doesn't have a one-size-fits-all solution, so even in the unlikely event that someone out there has it totally figured out, their systems may not suit you or your life. That's why you'll notice that in this book, I don't say things like "Turn off all text notifications"; instead, I tell you to turn off the text notifications that don't serve you.

---

22. One such high schooler, Adam Raine, died by suicide with ChatGPT's encouragement.
23. The first iPhone came out in 2007, followed by an Android smartphone (the HTC Dream) in 2008. Thus, smartphone use really accelerated in the 2010s.

A look back: The smoking analogy

Historically, when new things enter society, people look at the good, don't yet know about the bad, and go for it. Some wonder if this is currently happening with AI. I think this illustrates some really great characteristics of humanity: openness and optimism. But everything comes at a cost. Take smoking, for example. Cigarette smoking rose in the late 1800s due to the invention of cigarette rolling machines and advertising. Even with medical reports linking smoking to lung cancer beginning to appear in the 1920s, smoking's popularity continued to grow in the early 1900s due to continued marketing and the tobacco industry's ability to influence political policies. Advertising played a major role in people's adoption and continued use of cigarettes, despite more and more studies coming out that showed the negative health effects of smoking (both *argumentum ad populum* and mimetic desire are at play here).

Take Wayne McLaren from the "Marlboro Man," for example: an advertising campaign that has been studied extensively for its effectiveness. He was considered the epitome of masculinity, and many bought Marlboros to try to emulate him. He died of lung cancer at the age of 51 in 1992.

Emulating others, after all, is more fun than looking at the facts. Although reports popped up starting in the early 1900s linking smoking and lung cancer, the first total ban on smoking on flights didn't come until 1995. This is all to say that I wouldn't rely on policies to guide your personal decision-making.

Your attention has value, so somebody's profiting

When we lose, others gain

When we think about scrolling and unnecessary phone use, we often think about what the scrolling costs *us*: time that could be spent doing other things, stress or anxiety seeing what others have that we don't, impulse purchases, the toll of reading doom and gloom headlines... But most people don't consider who's profiting off our phone use.

We currently live in the "attention economy." This term was coined by Nobel Laureate Herbert Simon in the 1970s. Even before the birth of the internet (1983) or the iPhone (2007), Simon realized that we were moving from a materials-based economy to an attention-based one. You may also have heard the term "information economy." Simon argues that we live in an attention economy rather than an information economy, because information is endless but attention is finite. The resources that make up an economy must be finite in order to create scarcity, supply, and demand.

Your attention is currency

So, what does the attention economy have to do with your phone use? Attention is becoming more and more valuable. Your clicks and views have a dollar value, and companies and influencers are profiting off them. Have you ever considered how streaming services offer free or discounted versions of their services that include ads? These services aren't actually free or discounted. You're paying for them partly with money and partly with your attention, which these companies find just as valuable. (And marketing works on everyone.)

Why it hurts to watch others scroll mindlessly

If it ever bothers you when someone else is scrolling mindlessly, I think that the attention economy can help explain this. First, it can be annoying when you're spending time with someone and they pull out their phone (this is known as "phubbing," or "phone snubbing"). Even this can be traced to a transactional imbalance. There you are, giving your counterpart your undivided attention, and they're giving theirs to something or someone else. Naturally, the two most common responses are to feel annoyed or to take out your phone yourself ("If you're not paying attention to me, I'm not paying attention to you").

If you're in the position where you're the one who needs to address your phone, first I would ask yourself the question, "Can this wait?" And if the answer is no, acknowledge to the other person that you need to break away for a moment, and explain why. You wouldn't open a book mid-conversation with someone. It should be just as unacceptable to just take out your phone.

Even if you're not directly interacting with someone, it can be depressing to watch them scroll, especially when it's someone you care about. You're watching them lose a game that they don't even realize they're playing. It reminds me of watching someone play slots. Your attention is a finite resource that you can spend on yourself (doing something you enjoy, working toward a goal you care about), give to others (lend a listening ear to a friend, watch a movie with your kid that you may not be crazy about but that they're so happy to share with you), or give away to a stranger somewhere on the internet. I think being aware of these distinct possibilities, and intentionally choosing what you want to do with your attention, is a huge positive step.

Spend attention like you spend money

I'm not saying you should never scroll. I'm saying that when you do scroll, it should be because you want to, and only after you've considered how much you're paying for the scrolling.

Just as you usually take the monetary price into consideration when you purchase something, you should take the attention price into consideration when you decide to spend time scrolling. Maybe you'll come up with rules. Some people decide on a hard stop when they go into a casino: "I'll lose up to $100, and then I'll stop." Another common rule is to decide on a percentage of your income to use toward housing or vacations.

Some examples of scrolling rules are "I'll scroll for x number of minutes and stop" (for this, you can use a timer or a distraction blocker to help you) or "I never purchase something that an influencer advertises until I've let it sit in my cart for two days."

Why tech is so good at capturing your attention

Since companies and people want your attention, they've figured out how to manipulate you into giving them as much of it as possible. Just as a casino doesn't have windows so you don't know how much time is passing, or IKEA is a one-way maze that forces you to pass by every product before you check out, or grocery stores put yummy snacks by the checkout, tech companies use psychological tricks to keep you on your device longer. With social media, for example, you're motivated by intermittent reinforcement: when a desired behavior is rewarded randomly, the unpredictability of the rewards makes the behavior more tempting (a classic example is gambling). Apps are designed with intermittent reinforcement to keep you coming back, wondering if you'll get a funnier reel than the one you just watched.

Ask yourself: Who's profiting?

When I find myself on my phone, not quite sure if I should put it down, I try to ask myself, "Who's profiting?" A very typical outcome is that I profit first, for five seconds or so. Maybe I want to check the weather before I get dressed or send a happy birthday text to a friend. The tricky part is then ensuring I don't stay stuck on my phone and let others profit off me. Asking myself why I'm about to engage with my phone, and what I'm using it for, makes it easier to catch myself a couple of minutes later if I notice that I'm no longer the one profiting. So, remember to always ask: "Who's profiting?"

Avoid all-or-nothing thinking

Keeping your phone habits consistent despite life's changes is challenging. Sometimes, you may knowingly allow them to shift. That's completely okay. When you stay in a hotel room or at a friend's house, for example, you may have no choice but to have your phone in your room. And then, when you return home, your phone may creep back into your bedroom. Awareness is key. It's crucial not to define yourself by small, often temporary changes in your behavior. It's your overall habits that matter.

All-or-nothing thinking, or "black-and-white thinking," is something that none of us are immune to, and you probably fall into it unconsciously more frequently than you realize. When your coworker forgets to send you a report, you might think, "He *always* forgets to send that report to me." When you're contemplating a personal hero, you might think, "She *always* knows what to say and do." When you forget to put your phone outside of your bedroom at bedtime, then wake up and scroll, you might think, "I'll *never* remember to put my phone in the kitchen before bed."

All-or-nothing thoughts are dangerous, unhelpful, and almost always untrue. Our brains are constantly trying to find patterns so we can create shortcuts in our thoughts. For the most part, this is helpful. You don't need to look at the metal object on your bedside table every morning and think, "Could fit around my wrist, has numbers one through twelve, tells time... aha, a watch!" before putting it on. You just know that it's a watch, and you put it on. But in the case of all-or-nothing thinking, your brain is making a false generalization. Noticing when you make these sweeping conclusions can be helpful. Look out for words like "never" and "always" in your thoughts.

A man I was coaching was talking about how he was trying to keep his time on TikTok down, telling me that he had some good days, but some days he found himself on it for hours and hours. I sensed some all-or-nothing thinking when he seemed to categorize days as "good" or "bad" (with no in-between). I asked him to walk me through one of the "bad" days. He mentioned one common outcome: when he was cooking dinner after work, he'd scroll for a few minutes while waiting to flip over the chicken. At this point, he'd feel like he'd scrolled anyway, so he'd scroll while he ate, and then he'd scroll in bed.

Although he didn't realize it until we spoke, the time he spent scrolling while waiting for something to cook (usually less than 10 minutes) caused him to label that day as a "failure," and then he'd conclude that he might as well just scroll the rest of the night away. I pointed out that he could scroll while the chicken cooked, and then forget the time that's already occurred (a sunk cost); that way, he'd have the whole evening open to him to spend however he pleased. Scrolling while the food cooks doesn't dictate his behavior for the rest of the evening. When I followed up with him a couple of weeks later, he told me that the most useful part of our session was when I said, "Just because you wasted one hour scrolling doesn't mean you have to waste the next hour."

You're trying to make lasting, sustainable changes. You may surprise yourself with your ability to make dramatic changes easily, and you may also surprise yourself when a seemingly small adjustment trips you up over and over again. Give yourself grace. If the intention is there, and if you're reflective and honest with yourself in measuring your progress, you'll get to where you want to be. Noticing and identifying motivation slumps and all-or-nothing thinking will greatly speed up your progress and get you much further than you could've gone otherwise.

Every pickup is practice: Are you practicing presence or avoidance?

Every time you pick up your phone when you're having trouble concentrating on something, you're literally practicing not concentrating. You're giving your brain the okay to stop as soon as it's uncomfortable. It's a bit like coaching a runner, and every time they tell you they're getting tired, saying, "Okay, stop running and take a break." This is risky business. When you allow yourself to go on your phone when something's really hard, that becomes the new status quo. Then you might start zoning out on your phone when things get only moderately difficult. Before you know it, anytime there's a lull in your work, you'll be scrolling for half an hour.

Some clients have told me, though, that they don't even notice picking up their phone. They know they pick it up too frequently, and they've decided that one of their technophilosophies[24] is not to scroll when they're concentrating on something challenging. But they keep accidentally picking up their phone! In this case, they need to make it harder to pick up their phone. This could be as simple as putting it in another room when they're in deep work, or something a little more personalized, like turning off face ID to intentionally increase latency.

The good news is that just as reacting immediately to triggers is an easily learned habit, it's also an easily unlearned one. The first day will feel the most challenging and unnatural, but you'll quickly get used to the new normal.

And when the going gets tough, remind yourself that practice makes progress. Just as phone use begets more phone use, reading begets more reading, presence begets more presence, and so on. Breaking the initial inertia is the trickiest part.

Everyone has unique triggers

Boredom, mentally challenging situations, constant notifications, and other people's pickups are common triggers. But you may notice others of your own. Give yourself credit every time you notice; a change in behavior will quickly follow.

---

24. Your personal beliefs on how you want to interact with technology, including how you interact with your phone.

There are some situations that affect us all: constant notifications, social triggers, our phone's ease of access over other choices. But we also all have unique challenges. After our session together, Lucas (from Chapter 7 trimmed down his notifications and also decided to turn off work notifications after he was done with the workday, but he set aside half an hour at around 11 p.m. to go through the work messages that had come through in the evening before winding down for bed. This way, he didn't need to worry during the afternoon, as he knew he would get to the messages later.

TASK: Reflect and refine

What are your triggers? External triggers will be social (someone takes out their phone) and environmental (if you usually scroll when you hit the couch, hitting the couch will probably make you want to start taking out your phone).

Try to notice your internal triggers as well: boredom, escapism, avoidism. And remember, not all triggers are bad or avoidable; your goal is to be aware of them, so you understand why you do what you do and can have a say in how you respond to these triggers.

How to keep going

You'll probably have a smartphone for the rest of your life, even if you're no longer on track to spend 13 years of your life scrolling on it. (Congratulations, by the way.)

To stay on this new path, remember the three pillars:

1. Be kind to yourself
2. Design over willpower
3. Never leave a vacuum

If you keep these in mind, any slip back into unintentional scrolling is another opportunity to reflect, design, and reach a more deliberate relationship with technology.

> If you'd benefit from ongoing reminders, resources, and to stay in touch, visit howtostopscrolling.com.

You can find downloadable versions of all the worksheets and references at howtostopscrolling.com. Review them for examples, inspiration, and tactical tips on how others are managing their devices. And feel free to reach out and share your progress with me directly; you can email ruby@rubyrybawrites.com. Hope to hear from you soon.

Acknowledgements

Putting a book out into the world is no easy feat and I would never have been able to do it without the support of many incredible people.

First, I want to thank my husband Andrew, who has shown me unwavering support since I first had the idea to write a book, and who cheered me on as my enthusiasm and belief in myself ebbed and flowed.

Second, thank you to everyone who shaped me as a reader, learner, and writer. Thank you to my mom, Eriko Mercure, who taught me that to live is to read. Thank you to my dad, David Mercure, who taught me to always be curious. I am so lucky to have parents who have taught me and continue to teach me empathy, compassion, integrity, and perseverance. Thank you to my in-laws, Doctors Alexander and Krishna Ryba, lifelong learners and educators, who are always willing and active participants in my discussions on technology. Thank you to my influential teachers at Andover High School including Stacey Giggie who led me through *No Exit*, *The Metamorphosis*, and *Inferno*, Thomas Meyer who introduced me to Maslov's Hierarchy of Needs, and Scott Aubrey who taught me *A Tale of Two Cities*. Thank you to Dr. Anne Moore who assigned *Shitty First Drafts* as a reading assignment in a summer program when I was 15. Thank you to Dr. Jennifer Goldin who taught me much of what I know about psychology. And thank you of course to the authors of these works and all of the works I have read and yet to read.

Third, I want to thank everyone who supported this project. To Brian Hall for telling me very early on, that "the world needs this book," to Efthymios Philip Papageorgiou for reading every single draft I wrote, and many others including Mayra Florez, Aliza Sharfe, Candice Brinkman, and Shelly Covey.

Thank you to the team at Useful Books: Rob Fitzpatrick, Brian Hall, and Devin Hunt. Thank you for believing in me and in this book, for advising, mentoring, editing, designing, reading, re-reading, and re-reading again.

Thank you to all of my beta readers for taking time out of their lives to give me feedback including Efthymios Philip Papageorgiou, Nicholas Ryba, Christie Ryba, Leslie Schaller, Glenn Stovall, Neo Yee, Maxime Vachier-Lagrave, Yuanling Yuan, Justine Ramdas, Dustin Moy, Mike Miller, Ritavan, Ariya Zheng, George Kenefati, Laura Saracho, Amberley Tapp, Curt Sternum, Mark Weinart, and many more.

I also need to thank those who took wonderful care of my children while I worked. A mother cannot focus on creating, if her thoughts are with her children. Balancing working and mothering is nearly impossible, but my parents, in-laws, Alyssa Costa, Lillian York, Lealine Auger, and Jodie Johnson, made it possible.

And thank you, dear reader, for wanting to make positive change in this world by examining yourself and your habits. For deciding that you want to live your life to the fullest instead of wasting years away on your phone, and courageously acting upon that choice, so that others can learn from and follow you.

References

Chapter 1

- “5 hours and 16 minutes per day”: https://www.harmonyhit.com/phone-screen-time-statistics/
- “within 10 minutes of waking up”: https://www.reviews.org/mobile/cell-phone-addiction/
- “Impairments of focused attention”: https://pmc.ncbi.nlm.nih.gov/articles/PMC8204720/
- “Neck / back pain”: https://www.robinrecovery.com/post/addiction-to-cell-phone-statistics-and-facts
- “Twice as likely to have anxiety”: https://www.thetimes.com/uk/technology-uk/article/fifth-of-older-teens-have-problematic-reliance-on-phones-tmrthvdfc
- “Zombie scrolling syndrome”: https://www.newportinstitute.com/resources/mental-health/zombie_scrolling/
- “usage patterns predicted workplace stress”: https://arxiv.org/abs/1803.03863
- “normative dissociation”: https://arxiv.org/abs/2407.18803
- “more to do with the environment than the person”: https://pmc.ncbi.nlm.nih.gov/articles/PMC4070113/

Chapter 2

- "turning off autoplay": https://arxiv.org/abs/2412.16040

Interlude

- "on social media for 2.5 hours a day": https://www.bls.gov/news.release/atus.nr0.htm
- "high quality micro-breaks": https://pmc.ncbi.nlm.nih.gov/articles/PMC9432722

Chapter 7

- "switching between tasks can cost you": Meyer, D. E. & Kieras, D. E. (1997a). A computational theory of executive cognitive processes and multiple-task performance: Part 1. Basic mechanisms. Psychological Review, 104, 3-65.

Bonus chapter

- "Cigarette smoking rose in the late 1800s": Brandt AM. *The Cigarette Century: The Rise, Fall and Deadly Persistence of the Product that Defined America.* Basic Books. New York, 2007
- "marketing works on everyone": https://knowledge.insead.edu/marketing/think-youre-immune-advertising-think-again

Made in the USA
Monee, IL
04 November 2026

67380512R00075